Getting off the ground

Physical and outdoor education
as active life skills
for visually handicapped children and young people

Sue Walker

Dedication

Dedicated to the pupils and students, past and present,
of Dorton House School and Dorton College

© Sue Walker 1992

Published by
Royal National Institute for the Blind
224 Great Portland Street
London W1N 6AA

ISBN 0 901797 86 3
Printed by Vigo Press Ltd.

Price £8.50

Contents

Part Two

Taking visually handicapped children outdoors : some strategies
for increasing confidence, self-esteem and physical skills through
a wide selection of outdoor pursuits.

Part Three

The benefits and results of encouraging visually handicapped children to take part in physical activities. What does the future hold?

Foreword

This book is intended as a resource for teachers in mainstream and special schools. It provides information about physical education opportunities both indoors and out, for visually impaired children and young people. Recent research has indicated that there are at least 10,000 children in the UK between the ages of 3 and 18+ identified from local education authority records as having a visual impairment. (Blind and partially sighted children in Britain: The RNIB survey. Volume 2. HMSO, 1992) Other authors suggest the figure may be twice this size.

Increasingly, visually impaired children are being educated in ordinary mainstream schools alongside sighted pupils. This can pose a particular challenge for their teachers, many of whom will be unfamiliar with the special educational needs of a blind or partially sighted child. Few of these teachers will have had the opportunity to undertake specialist training.

We hope the ideas and examples in this book will do much to encourage visually impaired children's participation in a variety of sporting, leisure and outdoor activities, and through this, the development of a range of skills they will be able to use throughout adult life.

My thanks go to Dr Mike Tobin, Department of Education, University of Birmingham for encouraging Sue Walker to adapt and publish this MEd dissertation. Also grateful thanks to RNIB's Leisure team and the RNIB Publications Unit for their support and to Carol Lawrence who has typed this manuscript.

Louise R Clunies-Ross
Assistant Director, Education
Policy Development and Information Services

RNIB March 1992

Preface

Movement is considered to be an essential part of education for every child, and it is important for ensuring successful learning (White, 1980). Physical education is a foundation subject in the National Curriculum and is rightly part of every child's education.

During the last ten years there has been an increased awareness of the importance of health-related fitness and the relationship between activity levels and chronic illnesses (Woodhouse, 1988). Visually handicapped children, who tend to be less active than their sighted peers, require an even greater emphasis on education for an active adult life.

The aim of this book is to illustrate the ease with which visually handicapped children can be included in the wide spectrum of physical education and outdoor pursuits. The book is based on 18 years' experience of teaching physical education and outdoor activities to visually handicapped children, in both segregated and integrated situations. Its aim is to dispel any fears that mainstream physical education teachers might have about including blind and partially sighted children in physical activities.

Throughout the book, emphasis is placed on the vital contribution that physical education can make towards enabling all visually handicapped children to achieve the self-awareness and confidence needed to lead active, mobile lives in the sighted world, once they have left school.

Sue Walker
Dorton House School

Kent 1992

x

1

The meaning of visual handicap in school-age children

The term 'visual handicap' refers to those children

> 'who have difficulties in seeing which necessitates the use of special methods or adaptations to materials and who need to use special aids and equipment for learning.' (Chapman and Stone, 1988)

The amount of vision these children have will vary. Some will have sufficient sight to use print and to assist independent mobility. With the correct teaching methods, these children can learn in the same way as fully sighted children. Others, at the opposite end of the scale, will have light perception or no sight at all. Children's cognitive, linguistic, social and motor abilities are affected by substantially reduced or a total lack of vision.

There are many reasons for the visual problems observed among school age pupils. Major causes are congenital cataracts, optic nerve atrophy, and very short sight (myopia).

Most severely visually impaired children have some useful vision, and it is now well established that all these children must be encouraged to make use of whatever sight they have. Physical education can play an important part in encouraging visually handicapped children to use even the smallest amount of sight to improve confidence and mobility. Quite naturally, if they enjoy moving, visually handicapped children will use sight to increase their speed of progress, to find objects in the gymnasium more easily, to watch others or judge distances.

Many of the visually impaired children integrated into mainstream schools today have partial sight. This can mean that vision is only possible out of one or other of the eyes and images may be distorted, blurred or fragmented. Certain eye conditions reduce the field of vision and therefore many partially sighted children look at objects sideways, or have to wear thick glasses and use optical aids to read and travel about.

Partially sighted pupils, more than blind children often find the effort of keeping up with their sighted peers exhausting. As Corley (1989) states:

> 'Even with all the right aids and with good lighting, the effort required to read the amount of printed material at secondary

1

level is considerable and should not be underestimated.'

Mason and Tobin (1986) found the speed at which visually handicapped children processed visual information was generally well below that of the majority of sighted children. A study by Cowen and Bobgrove (1966), revealed that partially sighted children felt more rejected and pitied by their peers than did blind children. Psychological difficulties can arise in children with low vision who find they are unable to develop their self-concept as a result of insufficient visual feedback. This often leads to feelings of anxiety which then affects the whole of their development.

Eye conditions that put certain visually handicapped children at risk through physical education and outdoor activities

Most visually handicapped children will be able to take a full part in physical education and outdoor activities at school without further damaging their sight. Those who have to take extra care are few in number, but include those children with dislocation of the lens who need to be restrained from taking part in activities that might cause them to lose what little sight they have. Partial or total dislocation of the lens may be hereditary or may result from trauma. All contact sports must be avoided by these children so that they are removed from the likelihood of bumping or hitting their heads against others, apparatus or water (as when diving).

Very short sighted children, with high myopia, can run the risk of detaching their retinas. Similarly, children who have had cataracts removed are more prone to retinal detachment. Children with buphthalmos (large eye) have reduced fields of vision and are likely to increase the pressure in their eyes if they take part in diving, trampolining and contact sports such as football. Children with one eye should be carefully monitored to avoid any risk to their good eye, as should children with eye conditions such as vitreous retinopathy, a condition which causes the eyes to bleed.

It is important that all physical education teachers and other specialists who teach and organise physical activities for visually handicapped children have a complete understanding of the children's eye conditions. This does not require extensive medical knowledge, but rather a sound understanding of the problem and its relationship to all physical exercise. This is one example of an area where specialist physical educationists of visually handicapped children can pass on their experiences and expertise to others who have not obtained further qualifications but are teaching visually handicapped children in mainstream schools.

The role of physical education and outdoor activities for visually handicapped children and young people

Physical and outdoor education can play an important part in helping visually handicapped pupils to overcome a lack of confidence in themselves and also provide a channel for profitable integration. The aims of the physical education curriculum for children with special needs do not vary from the aims of all children. The difference comes in the objectives, which have to take into account any limitations imposed by these children's special needs. As Williams (1984) stresses, physical educationists need to understand the implications of visual handicap in order to plan suitable programmes for visually impaired children and not simply to give visually handicapped children a skeleton selection of the activities that sighted children are taught.

Frequently, visually handicapped pupils are found to be less fit than their sighted peers. They tend to be overweight, more sedentary and physically weaker, finding sustained exercise difficult to maintain. In 1986 Hanna came to this conclusion following Jankowski's 1981 report based on children attending a visually handicapped school in America. In comparison, this does not apply to many pupils at Dorton House School for the visually handicapped. At the time of writing, few who are currently attending the school could be classified as overweight or sedentary.

All physical education teachers know the importance of teaching pupils to enjoy and continue to take exercise as a life-skill, to fight against overweight, breathing difficulties and heart disease. The Vernon Report (1972) underlined the importance of visually handicapped people being as physically independent as possible if they are to 'play the fullest possible part in the community at large.'

Visually handicapped children often appear to be awkward and inhibited, frightened to move freely, apparently unaware of their body shape and its functional use. Cratty and Sams (1968) suggest that finding out about space is one of the most important problems a blind person has to solve. Difficulties in acquiring a concept of space are caused by immature spatial concepts and poor kinaesthetic senses.

Vision is considered to be one of the most important senses contributing to learning. The more visual experiences children have, the more their brains are stimulated, leading to a greater accumulation and variety of visual images and memories. Without body awareness, good posture and balance, visually handicapped children will have great difficulty in performing daily living skills and mastering efficient mobility techniques. This means that one of the most important aspects of physical education programmes for visually handicapped children is to build up, through activities, a steadily increasing love of freedom of movement. From this, body and spatial awareness should automatically be increased.

Visually handicapped children, both those who are blind and those who are partially sighted, can seem to be different from sighted children because of acquired mannerisms. These might be rocking, twisting, eye-poking or shaking and banging parts of their bodies. Resnick (1973) attributed these mannerisms to a lack of opportunities to experience natural movement.

Childhood is a time for discovery. Without physical exercise visually handicapped children can be deprived not only of physical development but also of mental stimulation. Physical education can reduce mannerisms in visually handicapped children by providing stimulation through movement and improved motor development which in turn is an important part of human development.

Palazesi (1986) emphasised the importance of any movement and motor development programme for visually handicapped children, providing them with 'a total awareness of body and space through movement'. Palazesi concentrated her study on pre-school children, but her conclusions are relevant to the movement education of all visually handicapped children.

Visually impaired pupils, especially those in mainstream schools who do not have the same opportunity to achieve success at sports as their sighted peers, can feel failure too easily. The same problem can arise in special schools for the visually handicapped which cater for both blind and partially sighted pupils. A partially sighted boy who was football captain in his special school, might not even play the game in his local comprehensive. A totally blind child in a class of partially sighted peers in a special school may feel left out if careful planning of lessons is not done before team games and other similar activities take place. Low self-esteem can result in the frustration and anxiety that are compensated for by outbursts of aggressive behaviour or periods of withdrawal, which are not easy to solve.

Withdrawal can take the form of refusing to answer questions or talk spontaneously, which is unnatural for visually impaired children. These pupils will often be found standing alone, exhibiting 'blind mannerisms' (that is, stereotyped behaviour), and waiting to be led by someone else. These children appear to have lost 'effective communication skills' (Harrell and Strauss, 1986) and to have acquired a learned helplessness. Aggressive outbursts usually occur when conversations break down after an unfavourable comment has been made, resulting in the pupil lashing out at anyone within striking distance. This action which is usually spontaneous, and can at times lead to physical damage, may often be attributed to loss of self esteem. Gurney (1988) emphasised the need for all children to be challenged and to take certain risks in order to help them to grow up with a high level of self-esteem. Physical education needs to be seen as part of the whole curriculum and to provide a quality of life that promotes self-esteem. Outdoor education can provide the challenge and stimulation that enhances the development of all children, especially those who are unable to take a full part in team games and other sports.

However, there is a danger that unless physical education programmes are designed carefully, some children especially girls, will opt out of physical activities altogether. Gould (1984) in America and Fox and Biddle (1988) in Britain, found this to be true with visually handicapped pupils. Arnold (1970) underlined the important part physical education has for the visually handicapped in bringing about a healthy and harmonious growth of individuals by paying attention to what pupils want to do, in choosing activities and in building up their self-esteem.

Physical education has an important part to play in assisting successful integration of visually handicapped pupils into mainstream schools. This is far more likely to be achieved if physical education teachers in mainstream schools have a good understanding of the movement difficulties visually handicapped pupils can experience and of the means of overcoming these difficulties.

Physical education influences the overall development of children: physically encouraging correct posture and fitness; psychologically instilling confidence and poise, alertness and vitality which offset frustration; and socially, in working with others, sharing responsibilities and experiencing leadership. Frostig and Maslow (1970) attribute the capacity of movement education to improving children's ability to learn academic subjects. Because of the nature of their special needs, visually impaired children need to experience physical education and outdoor activities as much, if not more often than, sighted children who can of course benefit from rapid acquisition of the basis of most physical activities visually. Visually handicapped children who feel safe and confident in physical activities will willingly share them with sighted children.

Understanding the movement problems of visually handicapped children

Poor motor control and difficulties in performing physical activities often begin in early childhood. Without sight, which attracts sighted babies to watch and move towards people and objects, blind babies receive less stimulus to encourage movement. The smallest amount of sight will lessen this problem, and most severely visually impaired children do have some useful vision. Lack of sight or limited vision accounts for the difference in motor development between blind and partially sighted children, to the extent that babies without sight are occasionally thought to be mentally retarded or to exhibit developmental delay when compared with their sighted peers.

Parents are the best educators of their young children. Often, parents of visually impaired babies are disillusioned by the lack of response on the faces of their children when they approach them. Visually handicapped children often listen with passive expressions on their faces and rarely turn their heads towards people who speak to them. Turning their heads would limit the sound input by covering one of their ears. This can be misinterpreted as disinterest and the parents experience fear and confusion at their children's lack of interest in them. Parents of blind babies generally pick their children up less frequently than they do sighted children. With reduced parental contact this results in an increased amount of time the children are left to amuse themselves which contributes to the development of mannerisms and methods of self-stimulation.

By contrast, all children in Africa and in most of the Third World are carried around on their mother's back - or the back of another female - for two years or more. Therefore from birth, visually handicapped babies in these societies involuntarily experience an adult's movements, such as walking, running, working and dancing. Without fear, these young children have explored the moving world long before they have learnt to walk by themselves. As a result, visually handicapped children in Africa rarely exhibit mannerisms, as they are infrequently left alone. When standing, these babies easily respond to suggestions of movement, especially when accompanied by music or drumbeats. Large families living in the same family compound provide all children, including those who are visually handicapped, with stimulation from other people. They naturally experience from the start the feeling of moving through space (Abang 1985). The author can substantiate Abang's conclusions, from personal studies of West African blind children over a number of years.

There are fewer opportunities for visually handicapped children in the West to experience moving through space. Sitting, crawling and walking are rarely learnt naturally. In addition to their delayed response to movement, Fraiberg (1977) found that blind babies were also delayed in their ability to respond to sounds. Visually handicapped babies do not like lying in the prone position, but choose to remain on their backs, kicking their legs, leaving their hands to lie idly beside them. Without encouragement to play with toys that require finger dexterity, or to turn onto their tummies to strengthen their necks and backs in preparation for crawling, visually handicapped children can grow up with weak and clumsy upper body movements, creating later problems with gross and fine motor skills that will affect mobility skills.

Visually handicapped children often stand with widely-spaced legs and turned-out feet. Later, this leads to an awkward gait and poor, round-shouldered posture. Physical exercise and day-to-day movement will become more tiring for blind children if early stimulation is not experienced and correct posture is not encouraged. Partially sighted children exhibit similar problems with their posture and gait. Learning to compensate and adjust to low vision results in incomplete concepts of how they should stand and move. Parents of partially sighted children are often less sympathetic to their children's difficulties than they are to those of children who are blind. Later this can lead to anxiety.

It is natural for parents with handicapped children to be fearful and want to protect them. However, overprotection can result in poor mobility and retarded physical development. For example, blind children may still be pushed around in a pushchair long after they are able to walk. This makes them stiff and reluctant walkers. In their study of the physical recreation of blind adults in the USA, Sherrill, Rainbolt and Ervin (1984) found that most of the visually handicapped people they asked valued physical education but found they had little opportunity to follow their schoolday interests. They blamed parental over-protection in their early years.

Parental over-protection of visually handicapped children increases the difficult task for physical education teachers, who have to spend many years proving to these children and their parents that movement is enjoyable and well within the children's capacities.

The relationship between physical education and mobility for visually handicapped children

Physical education and mobility skills are very closely linked. Before a visually handicapped child is ready to use a long cane, many of the techniques needed to master their skill efficiently can be learnt in the context of physical education.

Tooze (1981) clearly states how the physical education programme is directed towards the enjoyment of movement. If visually handicapped children feel confident and at ease moving around at home, at school and in the extended environment, formal mobility training will become far less of a burden. All visually handicapped children need to be encouraged to explore the environment by using their other senses of hearing, smell and touch to find the clues from which they can orientate themselves.

These skills can be developed through sound games and exercises, for example by listening to the bounce of a ball in order to catch it on the rebound, by tracking a moving object or running towards a constant sound. Visually handicapped children can increase their body awareness in the gymnasium by climbing over or under apparatus, swinging on ropes, going up wall bars or crawling through tunnels. Body planes and levels can be explored through dance. Parts of their bodies can be named or felt and touched in rhythmic games or movement exercises. All this increases their sense of laterality and directional ability. If visually handicapped children can enjoy moving in a creative way whatever their additional disabilities might be, throughout their lives they will move with confidence and be able to enjoy life far more.

It is important to help parents of blind children to encourage early motor skills and to allow safe exploration of the environment. This will increase the chance of their children growing up with good mobility and orientation skills. Visually handicapped children's posture and spatial awareness give a very clear idea of their later potential for good mobility. The earlier a visually handicapped child is encouraged to construct a mental map of the environment, the greater the chance that these aims can be realised.

It is vital that physical educationists understand the close links between physical education and mobility so that all visually handicapped children whether at mainstream or special school, can maximise their chances of becoming confident, mobile adults.

Further reading

Abang, T B (1985) 'Blindism : Likely Causes and Preventative Measures' Journal of Visual Impairment and Blindness, 79, 11, 400-401

Arnold, P J (1970) 'Physical Education, Creativity and the Self-Concept' Bulletin of Physical Education, 8, 1, 15-19

Chapman, E K and Stone, J (1988) The Visually Handicapped Child in Your Classroom London : Cassell

Corley, G Robinson, D and Lockett, S (1989) Partially Sighted Children Windsor : NFER-Nelson

Cowen, E L and Bobgrove, P H (1966) 'Marginality of Disability and Adjustment' Perceptual and Motor Skills, 23, 25, 869-870

Cratty, B H and Samms, T A, (1968) 'The Body Image of Blind Children' American Foundation for Blind Research Bulletin, 17

Department of Education and Science (DES) (1972) The Education of the Visually Handicapped (Vernon Report). London : HMSO

Fox, K and Biddle, S (1988) 'The Child's Perspective in Physical Education Part 2:Children's Participation Motives' British Journal of Physical Education, 19, 2, 79-82

Fraiberg, S H (1977) Insights from the Blind New York : Basic Books

Gould, D (1984) 'Psychosocial Development and Children's Sport' In: Thomas, J R (ED) (1984) Motor Development During Childhood and Adolescence. Minneapolis:Burgess

Gurney, P W (1988) Self-Esteem in Children with Special Educational Needs London : Routledge

Hanna, R S (1986) 'Effects of Exercise on Blind Persons' Journal of Visual Impairment and Blindness, 80, 5, 722-725

Harrell, R L and Strauss, F A (1986) 'Approaches to Increasing Assertive Behaviour and Communication Skills in Blind and Visually Impaired Persons' Journal of Visual Impairment and Blindness 80, 6, 794-798

Janowski, L W and Evans, J K (1981) 'The exercise capacity of Blind Children' Journal of Visual Impairment and Blindness, June 248-251

Palazesi, M A (1986) 'The Need for Motor Development Programs for Visually Impaired Preschoolers' Journal of Visual Impairment and Blindness, 80, 2, 573-576

Resnick, R (1973) 'Creative Movement Classes for Visually Handicapped Children in a Public School Setting' New Outlook for the Blind, 67, 442-447

Sherill, C Rainbolt, W and Ervin, S (1984) 'Physical Recreation of Blind Adults : Present Practices and Childhood Memories' Journal of Visual Impairment and Blindness, 78 10, 367-368

2

Physical education for young visually handicapped children and its relationship to pre-formal mobility skills

When young visually handicapped children start school, they will already have had varying experiences of movement. With specific teaching and carefully structured programmes, physical education can become a very important key to their full development, which includes increasing physical fitness and encouraging their concept of 'self'. At this early stage it is vital that parents and teachers work closely together to encourage active play both at home and at school, reinforcing activities and movement skills. It has been said that money spent on physical development of children with special needs is always money well invested; Rozzell (1987) estimated that for each child up to £1,000 can be saved 'in having to care for their every need in later life'.

Today, there is an increasing emphasis on providing all children from an early age with physical activities that are enjoyable and which enable them to develop skills and leisure interests that will be with them for the rest of their lives.

Young visually handicapped children must be actively encouraged to explore the world they live in as they do not instinctively move to explore an environment they cannot see. Cratty and Sams (1968) wrote that

> 'Freedom to explore and move about are indispensable for providing a range and variety of experiences necessary for all facets of development'.

Visually handicapped children who are encouraged to move freely develop their kinaesthetic senses. This can be achieved by exploring space with their limbs. Spatial orientation will also be increased if these movements are linked with verbal cues from parent or teacher. To increase the possibilities of successful mobility and a life-time love of physical activity, from the moment they start school visually handicapped children should be introduced to gymnastics, small apparatus and ball handling skills, movement awareness, suitable minor games and if possible, water play and swimming.

Young visually handicapped children, whether in special or mainstream schools, will be able to follow the main theme approach of modern educational gymnastics with ease, provided they are given whatever extra assistance they need. Some may have severe motor learning difficulties which are a direct result of lack of stimulation in their pre-school years. Children with motor learning difficulties naturally try to avoid situations where they are unable to succeed. In addition, visually handicapped children tend to avoid movement because they are unaware of the excitement and pleasure it can give them until they have tried different tasks. Their motor difficulties are increased because they are not stimulated by seeing others complete and enjoy physical activities. Initially, physical education teachers need to understand each child's individual needs and work closely with other members of staff as well as with the child's parents in order to overcome whatever specific difficulties a child may have.

Visually handicapped pupils in a gymnastics class in school will need to be shown apparatus and have movements and actions carefully described before beginning to use any of the equipment. In a mainstream school, visually impaired pupils will benefit from being given the opportunity to become familiar with the apparatus beforehand.

The teacher needs to address comments to all visually handicapped children by first attracting their attention by using each child's name. Children must be spoken to personally, as head gestures or eye contact are of course no use to anyone with a visual disability. When working in a group with sighted children, it is important for the physical education teacher to remember to address the visually impaired child directly, and never to talk 'at' a visually handicapped child 'through' another group member. This 'does he take sugar?' syndrome which has been noted in recent literature must be avoided at all costs.

Suitable words and use of tones and depths in speech patterns can increase the understanding of tension and shape, so easily recognised by sighted children. Teachers should not be afraid of using sighted words, as visually handicapped children are growing up in a sighted world in which they need to appreciate sighted concepts in order to have a greater understanding of the world they live in.

In most gyms and halls, because of their design, sounds can become distorted. Also younger children naturally make noise when they are enjoying themselves. However, it is important that the noise level never gets out of control and that there is absolute quiet when instructions are being given. In a mainstream sighted class, this will benefit the whole group, not only the visually handicapped children.

The responsibility for visually handicapped children in a mainstream gymnastics class must always lie with the teacher; but it is unrealistic to expect the physical education teacher to devote the whole lesson to the visually handicapped children, who might only be one or two in number. Sighted children in the class will willingly share the guiding of visually handicapped pupils over apparatus if introduced to the technique carefully and if they are not over-burdened with the task. In a class of visually handicapped pupils, the teacher cannot spend most of the lesson time with the totally blind children; however, if they are shown the task to be done carefully, they can be left alone to complete it, provided the teacher is constantly watching for possible problems and also talks continually, so that all the class know where the teacher is and what the rest of the group are doing.

In a mainstream school, and certainly in most special schools or units, visually handicapped children will have a resource teacher or classroom assistant(s). The presence of these helpers can be a valuable asset in physical education lessons. It is very easy to show a helper how to watch and assist visually handicapped children in a sighted group without the children feeling in any way inhibited. Alternatively, the helper can keep an eye on the main part of the class while the teacher gives the visually handicapped children some individual attention. In a special class, where the whole group benefit from individual stimulation and encouragement, an extra pair of hands is a bonus. In picture 1 a child helps a blind classmate adapt to the right position for a forward roll on the mats. Mainstream teachers who are unused to having assistance in lessons should learn to welcome the opportunity and, at times, insist upon it.

Picture 1. Forward roll on the gym mat

Apparatus and equipment

Apparatus in gymnastics lessons needs to be imaginatively arranged and to remain in the same place for more than one lesson, so that visually impaired children can become familiar with the layout. Partially sighted children will benefit from brightly coloured mats that differ from the colour of the floor, and planks, soft-topped tables and benches can also be obtained in contrasting colours. Contrast in texture of the top of different large pieces of apparatus will also assist the totally blind children to recognise and remember major features such as the length of certain benches and the distance of the soft-topped table from the ground in comparison with the hard flat box. Coloured mats will help partially sighted children judge the distance to the ground when they are stepping and jumping. Visually handicapped children can enjoy jumping off benches and boxes just as much as sighted children; some may require a helping hand at first, while others will be impatient to repeat the task. Picture 2 shows two visually handicapped children working with a large, soft ball in the gymnasium.

Picture 2. Working with the ball in the gymnasium

As with any activity in the gymnasium, it is important to have clear rules which all the pupils understand and carry out promptly. 'Stop' means 'stop.' This ends many situations which could result in visually handicapped children bumping into each other, into sighted class members or objects when they become disoriented. Most of the problems that arise in large spaces with visually handicapped pupils will become apparent when the group is moving freely around the floor over apparatus. It may be necessary in these circumstances to supervise the visually handicapped children in a sighted class closely, or indeed those with little or no sight in a special class.

Small apparatus should also be brightly coloured. It is important to remember the value of the colour and light reflecting off apparatus, as with toys, when obtaining materials for visually handicapped children. Rings, hoops, skittles and bats, rackets or sticks can all be obtained in deep, bright colours. It is useful to have a selection of different-sized balls. These are invaluable for throwing, catching and kicking practice and do not hurt if they should accidentally hit a child. (Special care must be taken in developing ball skills with children who have brain injuries or delicate eye conditions.) Visually handicapped children can learn to bounce and catch ordinary balls. They have to be reminded to keep their heads up and to let a hard ball return to their hands and not to bend down to meet it. Partially sighted children will be able to see a ball approaching but if they, like blind children, also listen to the timing of the throw or bounce of the rebound, their catching will be more accurate. Totally blind children can catch balls without an initial bounce, provided they are told when the ball is being released and the throw is very accurate and not too hard.

It is useful to have some balls with ball-bearings inserted through the valves. (Corley et al., 1989). This is an easy way of converting ordinary plastic balls for use by visually handicapped children. When the original valve has either been removed or pushed into the ball, ball-bearings can then be inserted and a new valve put into place. (Certain firms will do the task on request, but this means buying a large number of balls at once.) The ball-bearings rattle when the ball is thrown, bounced or rolled, but of course they make the ball heavier and less stable and therefore more difficult to manoeuvre. However, these balls are ideal for rolling along the ground, and they are an excellent means of encouraging the sense of sound location. The Royal National Institute for the Blind (RNIB), sells a rubber ball with bells inside it. Again, this is heavy and mainly suited to rolling. Footballs that have a bleeper inserted which is triggered off by pulling a cord, can also be obtained. These are durable and stand up to kicking or throwing, but they are rather heavy for younger children to use.

Soft, yellow tennis-sized balls can be hit by most partially sighted children. Some will need a slightly larger soft ball, allowing them to be introduced to racket or stick games. Totally blind children enjoy the texture of foam balls and they can become very skilled at passing them around their bodies. This increases spatial awareness and laterality. Fine motor control is encouraged, as fingers have to work hard to keep the ball in contact otherwise it will be lost.

Young blind children need plenty of opportunities to climb, swing, jump, crawl, twist, turn, roll, skip and hop. In fact, they need to be encouraged to be as active as sighted children. Tasks may take longer to master, but unless there are severe additional problems none of the full range of activities open to sighted children is beyond the scope of a visually handicapped child.

For visually handicapped children to move with skill and effectiveness they need first to understand their own bodies and the relationship of their body parts. An awareness of body image can be encouraged through all movement experiences. For example, music and movement provide an excellent means of developing kinaesthetic sense, and dance can give visually handicapped children experiences in orientation and mobility skills, both of which will also improve daily living skills. Visually handicapped children enjoy moving to music and they are often above average at making up rhymes and patterns of sound with their own voices or instruments. Increased sound or depth of tone will emphasise large and weighted movements while soft extended sounds increase stretching and turning. To a sighted child, these actions are very natural and obvious. To a blind child, they often have to be taught, but once the links have been learnt, the child will become more aware of his or her body and its function in movement and space.

Language and physical education

Language is an important part of teaching the visually handicapped, as it is with all children. Physical education is a very good way of extending children's concepts of time, space and weight, reinforcing the meaning of a word or phrase whilst the children are performing the movement. During movement and dance lessons, visually handicapped children can gain a greater concept of direction, level, speed and shape. This will benefit their understanding in other subjects such as mathematics. Above all, these are concepts that are essential for a confident understanding of orientation.

As a rule, visually handicapped children are unable to learn from watching others. It is therefore very important to develop the use of language and encourage it in play and physical activity. By verbalising while performing basic movements, physical education can assist visually handicapped children to learn more quickly. At first, all children talk to themselves while they are moving: 'I am crawling under this bench', 'climbing up the wall bars', 'putting the bean bag into the hoop.' The next stage is to think silently while moving. This process helps all children to perform, understand, order and control positive thinking.

Early mobility skills

Many visually handicapped children, walk and run awkwardly. They need to be taught to move well and maintain a good posture, so that mobility skills will be easier to master and they become less tired. As many different ways as possible should be found to encourage children to perform locomotive movements. Movement lessons out of doors should make use of natural banks, different textures of paths and the contrasting feel of grass and concrete, steps and slopes.

Activities out-of-doors

All children benefit from a good walk. Visually handicapped children, especially the youngest in school may not have had the chance to walk regularly. Whether the school is in an urban or rural area there are innumerable things to describe, listen to, touch and remember during a walk.

It is during these walks that young visually handicapped children can learn to 'trail', by stroking and touching walls and doors as they pass. Trailing is a technique used by visually handicapped people to follow guidelines by tracing a hand along the surfaces of different features as they pass by. Children can discover and become used to different surfaces when they are out on a location walk. Buildings, fences, doorways and walls can all become familiar landmarks after a while.

It is possible to use sound cues whilst on a walk. A fountain in the middle of a lily-pond that is surrounded by grass and a circular concrete path, can be negotiated by 5 year old blind children without help. With practice, they learn to keep the constant sounds of the fountain at a certain distance from them whilst walking in a circle round the pond. They will use the contrast of the path with the grass surround to guide them. The sun can also be of use. On a circular route the sun will be felt in one position on their heads and will appear to complete a full turn round them, until they end up where they started, with the sun again felt in the same position on their heads.

Orientation is the 'ability to locate oneself in spatial terms and to construct a mental map of the environment' (Chapman and Stone, 1988). Many games and play activities at school and in the local environment can be put to excellent use during physical education sessions, all the time increasing the confidence that will be needed for later independent travel using a long cane.

Where the children are in a mainstream school it may be unrealistic to take the whole group out at once, for a descriptive walk. This is another occasion where an additional helper is an advantage; perhaps a member of staff, a parent, local sixth-formers from a mainstream school or a voluntary helper. This is an excellent way of integrating small groups of sighted and visually handicapped children, as the sighted ones describe what they see and the blind children what they hear. It is surprising how many sounds sighted children miss until they are consciously made to listen!

Games

Visually handicapped children can be introduced to minor games which can be enjoyable and great fun. In a sighted situation, visually handicapped children in a large class can take part in all the skill practices that are built up before a full game of football, netball or rounders is played. All physical educationists are familiar with the latest emphasis on games teaching in schools. Gone are the days when the elite played in school teams to the boredom, frustration and sense of failure for the rest of the group. These children still play in teams, but greater emphasis is laid on 'the rest' which includes the visually handicapped children.

Games that encourage functional movement and body position, such as 'Simon says', are useful for understanding more about spatial awareness. All games that help visually handicapped children to identify parts of their bodies and locate sounds are important.

Visually handicapped children are frequently unable to move forward in straight lines. Fear of moving quickly into an empty space can also make their movements stilted and jerky. Confidence is built up between the teacher and the children so that a sound from a voice or clapping and banging, with extra encouragement, enables the children to run towards the noise at speed. Running up a grass bank strengthens legs and makes knees bend. Going down a bank teaches visually handicapped children how to alter their weight and centre of gravity to keep their balance. Paths can make good tracks that give some confidence when walking along, and these also encourage children to walk in a straight line. Games can be invented which require movement from one surface to another. The idea of camps or journeys through jungles and swamps adds variety to this early mobility training. Opportunities for invention are endless.

Soft-play areas/equipment

Movement and action can be achieved spontaneously if visually handicapped children have access to a soft-play area. The brightly coloured shapes that can be put together to form pools and swamps, tunnels, stairways and slides attract even totally blind youngsters. The feel of the smooth, shiny surfaces makes rolling, crawling, sliding, climbing and jumping a pleasure. At first, it is essential for the children to be closely supervised to avoid clashes and to encourage the most timid to explore. If a group of children are mixed, the sighted must be responsible for moving out of the way of their visually handicapped classmates. If the group are all visually handicapped, it is advisable to restrict the numbers of children working in a soft-play area to a suitable limit for comfort and safety. It can be daunting for a blind child to be knocked or bumped by surprise. Too many instances of this will counteract the benefit of working in this safe area and will begin to undermine the confidence that children build up within a soft-play area.

Soft-play rooms are expensive and beyond the reach of most mainstream schools. Alternatively, an area of mats pushed together to make a 'carpet' can create an excellent activity space. Visually handicapped children can roll and step, run, crawl and jump without fear of coming unexpectedly into contact with an obstacle. At first they need to be introduced to the shape and size of the mat area, and their movements initially need to be controlled to avoid misjudging the edges. Children who are hesitant can work closely with the teacher or another sighted or more adventurous member of the group. They can chase each other around, either crawling or moving on their feet. Two totally blind children can work together, remaining in contact with each other through speech and perhaps by using a rope. By keeping the tension tight, they know exactly how far apart they are and any alteration in the rope will need adjustment. A further guideline to signal the edge of the area can easily be created by putting a surround of different textured mats at the perimeter.

Rebound tumbling on a trampoline, aerobic table or bouncy castle is another activity that naturally teaches balance and flexibility. Visually handicapped children enjoy working on a full sized trampoline and even when they are very young their thrill at initiating movement this way is evident. It is essential to be in contact with them either by holding hands or using a belt on or off the trampoline. Soon, they will be able to jump on their own, with the normal safety precautions being carried out.

Encouraging free movement, linked with excitement and fun, is the best means of developing confidence in visually handicapped children. Working on smooth blocks and rebound surfaces can achieve this aim simply and effectively.

Water-play

Visually handicapped children enjoy water play. This is also an excellent way of involving both sighted and blind children. Visually handicapped children may need extra assistance at first, with someone in the water beside them. They will not be able to separate the different sounds in a large public or school bath, which can be very frightening, they need to be in constant contact with the teacher or a helper so that they do not feel lost. Apart from this, they will learn to swim in the same way as sighted children. It may take longer and they will have to be shown physically what their arms, body and legs should be doing. Older junior-aged children, when they are tall enough to stand confidently in the shallow end of a pool, can support a visually handicapped class member. This may mean holding onto them by the hands or waist, or swimming beside them.

Visually handicapped children need to swim as much as any other children. Swimming is one sport that blind and partially sighted people can share with sighted people. Once children can swim, they are able to take part in the full range of water sports when they get older.

Picture 3. Visually impaired children with an adult beside them in the water

Posture

Young visually handicapped children need to be encouraged at all times to stand up straight, to walk with long strides, to swing their arms and, if necessary, to hold up their heads and stop the rocking movements many tend to adopt if left on their own. It seems a long list, but it is an essential one if the children are going to grow up to be confident, mobile adults and able to hold their own in society. Physical education is a vital contributor to this process and at the same time provides an excellent way of counteracting what might otherwise develop into a life-long slouch, by increasing poise and functional motor performance.

Further reading

Chapman, E K and Stone, J (1988) The Visually Handicapped Child in Your Classroom, London: Cassell

Corley, G et al (1989) Partially Sighted Children, Windsor NFER-Nelson

Cratty, B H and Sams, T A (1968) 'The Body Image of Blind Children' American Foundation for the Blind Research Bulletin, 17

Rozzell, D (1987) 'Playing for the Future' Special Children, 11, 12-1

3

Physical education for older visually handicapped children

Introduction

Older visually handicapped children require a full and active physical education programme throughout their time at school, 'because of their tendency to be less active than their sighted peers, they need physical activities to avoid the poor muscle tone, poor posture and obesity that are too often present in visually impaired students.' (Scott, 1982)

The needs of this age group differ slightly from those of younger visually impaired pupils, as they do with sighted teenagers. This is the stage when account should be taken of individual likes and dislikes. As children mature into adults, experiences they have had when they were younger enable them to make a more informed choice, and by choosing certain activities, they are of course more likely to continue to enjoy these throughout their lives.

Apart from an awareness of movement difficulties resulting from inexperience and poor motivation when they were younger, visually handicapped teenagers are also more aware of the social aspects of their handicap. Without careful monitoring by physical educationists, many visually handicapped pupils - especially those in mainstream schools - can reject efforts to make them understand and enjoy the thrill of being physically active. Without creative, imaginative planning and teaching of physical education, visually handicapped children will have fewer chances than their sighted peers to become active and well coordinated. Pupils who achieve competence in an activity will usually experience a growth in overall self-confidence which in turn leads to the development of positive attitudes towards physical activity in the future.

Physical education teachers who work with older visually handicapped children in both special and mainstream schools need to concentrate on creating positive lines of communication between themselves and the pupils. Older children are far quicker to jump to conclusions over hastily-made statements. For example, an incorrectly phrased sentence, thoughtless side-remarks or undue sternness or anger can be blown up out of all proportion by visually handicapped pupils. Research has identified that some partially sighted children can experience teasing or taunts from their sighted peers. In physical education lessons it is important that teachers understand these potential difficulties and are ready to counteract any major problems that might arise from teasing. While sighted children can see from

23

a teacher's eyes and gestures that the sternness or joke need only be taken superficially, it is impossible for visually handicapped pupils to do this, therefore great care must be taken by teachers when they make casual comments or 'jokes' in their lessons.

The physical education programme

The greatest difficulty perceived by physical education teachers in mainstream schools and to a lesser extent, by those in special schools, during gymnastics lessons for older visually handicapped children is undoubtedly linked to heights. Seeing a blind child climbing up wall bars, using trampetts and vaulting tables, or working on high ladders and bars can be daunting. It is again at these times that sighted help can be used. In a mainstream class, other pupils are quite capable of working alongside a visually handicapped pupil. In a special school where it is rare to have large

Picture 4. Using exercise bicycles

classes pupils can, if necessary, work in pairs. Often a less able sighted or partially sighted child can gain a great deal of confidence by assisting a severely visually handicapped classmate. All children, with or without a disability, will enjoy physical activity far more if individual success can be ensured. Attitudes in the physical education profession now favour promoting health-related fitness and child-centred movement programmes which are ideal for visually handicapped children. Fitness is of course an essential component in successful mobility training. Many visually handicapped people have to walk many miles, and unless they are always taken by someone in a car to their destination, walking will become a major part of their lives. With poor sight, travelling on public transport is also strenuous and requires sustained stamina.

Whilst at school, pupils' fitness training can take the form of circuit activities in the gymnasium. Moving over, under, up, down and through apparatus tests everyone. The time factor involved in completing tasks is immaterial provided each individual works to improve personal targets. General fitness and opportunities for competition can also be achieved through circuit training.

Visually handicapped pupils of all ages benefit from the chance to use fixed activity machines. Exercise bicycles, rowing machines, rebound tables, walking or running machines, fixed weights, ski-training rocker platforms and so on can instantly give visually handicapped children a chance to compete with themselves and others. Whilst using fixed machines, a blind pupil can be left to work independently. As some mainstream schools will not have access to all of the equipment usually found in special schools for visually impaired pupils, this is an occasion when physical educationists can look to the community where there is an increasing emphasis, especially in urban areas, on providing physical activities outside school.

Local Sports Halls and Leisure Centres are being used by many schools as a major option with older children. While sighted children are playing squash, badminton or table tennis, visually handicapped pupils and others, can use the well-equipped gymnasia and weight-training rooms. Blind children are seen using exercise bicycles in picture 4.

Mainstream physical educationists automatically introduce sighted children to clubs and societies outside school. It is important that they know where to turn to so that visually handicapped children can have similar opportunities. This is where contact with specialist physical education teachers for the visually handicapped in special schools will help.

Visually handicapped boys find weight training and weight lifting a challenging activity and some girls also enjoy using weights, but to a lesser extent. Boys are able to master the techniques of lifting both light weights in the 'Clean and Jerk' class and heavier weights in 'Olympic' weight lifting to the standard of competing with the sighted. Recent observations by Allen (1988) showed that

> 'The feeling of 'being strong' has always been an important part of the self-concept amongst adolescent schoolboys, and more recently girls too have shown an increasing interest in personal body shape and the development of good muscle tone'.

Visually handicapped girls can use aerobic weights and body building exercises. Aerobic and fitness exercises provide an excellent form of integrated activity as there need not be extensive movement around an open space. Disco dance is enjoyed by all visually handicapped children and they can learn steps which enable them to build up routines, learnt also by the sighted pupils. Discos provide a social outlet for every member of the school, encouraging positive integration.

The gymnasium can also be used for ball games. Visually handicapped pupils can be introduced to basket ball and goal-ball skills which will improve and coordinate their understanding of ball games in general. Building from skills learnt at junior school, visually handicapped children can learn to shoot baskets and move more confidently about the court in response to sound cues. In Israel, many basket ball courts will be outside which minimises echo rebound, and the Israelis bang the rim of a basket ball goal to give blind children a point to aim at. In gyms or sports halls the sharp ring of the goal rim can become distorted. It is preferable to bang the rim with a wooden stick rather than a metal one, but also to coach shooting through technique and feel, to avoid too much sound location being needed.

Goal-ball is an exciting game, and there will be times when sighted or partially sighted group members will enjoy sharing a game with blind players. In a game of goal-ball everyone is totally blind, either naturally or by the use of a blindfold. The court is roughly the size of a badminton court and the ball is rolled between two goals by a team of two players. Shooting and defending requires skill and expertise. Goal-ball is played at both national and international level.

Judo is another activity that visually handicapped and sighted pupils can take part in on an equal basis. Judo requires contact with an opponent and it is ideally suited to both blind and partially sighted children.

Team games

To a great extent, field games obviously exclude many visually handicapped pupils. Skills practices and small games that are used to teach techniques will, however, be well within their grasp. While football, rugby, netball or lacrosse are being played in a mainstream school, the visually handicapped pupils in the group would be better off running or doing another physical activity that is timetabled for another group of sighted pupils. Generally,

26

there is at least one sighted pupil who is 'off games' for one reason or another and he or she could be profitably employed in guiding the visually handicapped children on a jog or walk, or assisting with individual ball skill practices.

Visually handicapped pupils take part in team games by learning to understand the principles of the game. They can learn to score and write up reports on games or become managers. Even so, it is important that they do not opt for static pastimes: visually handicapped pupils need to be active and remain physically fit.

As Brown wrote in 1987,

> 'Games are much more fun: they are an important medium for the achievement of educational goals in physical, psychological, social and emotional areas.'

Adapted games for the visually handicapped are simple to organise. Football can be played with a ball that makes a sound. At Dorton House School and RNIB New College, Worcester, purpose-built, enclosed hard areas are used for playing ball games. With metre-high sounding boards around the area, the ball rebounds with a noise and the high walls keep the ball in play. All mainstream schools have tennis and netball courts. It would be possible for one of these to be turned into a play area for visually handicapped pupils if the policy of the school is to include and to integrate visually handicapped children. There are many less able sighted boys and girls who would prefer to play a slower game with the visually handicapped members of the group than be shouted at and possibly demoralised by others in a full and fast game.

A totally blind child who is to play football with sighted or partially sighted pupils can similarly 'get in the way'. If he can be linked physically to a sighted partner, the two can play as one. The sighted boy can see the ball to receive it and his visually handicapped partner can be told where to pass it to. The game must not be a fast one, but a great deal of success is possible if the group is well prepared beforehand. The rules have to be adapted to ensure the ball is not passed directly at players' heads and faces and a brightly coloured ball is a great asset. Corley et al., (1989) describe how a partially sighted girl in a mainstream school became part of the netball team. Her height made her an excellent goal defence and she was told when to raise her arms to block a pass into the circle by another member of the team.

Many visually handicapped boys have a life-long love of cricket. Listening to the cricket commentary on the radio gives them hours of pleasure. Adapted cricket for visually handicapped people is played with a larger ball that rattles as it is rolled. The rules of the game are adapted to allow blind and partially sighted team members in the side to play an equal part.

Small, 'potted' games can be played by all children. Many of these games are easy to learn and others can be created by different groups. The emphasis is on team spirit, challenge and achieving success. Increasingly, more child-centred activities are being used in both junior and senior schools to minimise the chance of putting children off team games for the rest of their lives.

Certain visually handicapped children in special schools can also at times feel left out; but with a child-centred philosophy in the physical education department, this will never happen. Brown (1987), explains it this way

> 'The new challenge facing the physical education profession is to integrate these atypical children within the programme and ensure that the children not only achieve success but feel that they are being successful.'

Field events

Athletics is also perfectly within the reach of visually handicapped children. Pupils can attempt all the disciplines, provided they are given expert guidance. Totally blind children can run towards a caller, alongside others or against the clock. On longer distances they can run beside a partner who is calling them or who is in contact via a short length of rope. It is of course necessary to practise this technique before a race. The two runners must be equally matched and the sighted partner must not pull their blind companion along. This technique is well illustrated every year by paired runners in the London Marathon. Partially sighted pupils can run independently, especially if the track lines are broad and bright. To have raised guide lines for visually handicapped runners hampers both sighted and partially sighted athletes, but they can be of value at club level in events designed especially for blind people.

All the field events that interest children can be attempted. Obviously the javelin, shot and discus events can be dangerous, but in carefully controlled groups, constantly supervised by a member of staff, they are feasible. Without these precautions, however, they can be potentially lethal. Long and high jump for visually handicapped pupils need not be adapted, except that severely visually impaired children prefer a wider take-off board for long jump which is brightly painted at the edge. Blind children often choose to use standing or very short take-offs for both long and high jump. It takes hours of practice to master a perfect run-up. Visually handicapped pupils also enjoy cross-country running. In this activity it is important that a pupil with very limited or no sight is linked to a responsible partner. Preferably, the course should not, at first, contain too many hazards. Fields and grass banks or roads and paths are ideal. Trees can be negotiated provided they are not too close together, by following a rope guide line.

As with younger visually handicapped children, older pupils can gain a great deal from a good walk. Without having to concentrate of formal mobility

Picture 5. Walking with friends

skills, the companionship gained from walking with friends is highly beneficial. At the same time ecology, archaeology, nature and environmental studies can be discussed. Picture 5 shows a group of friends enjoying a walk along a woodland track in the Kent countryside.

Water-based activities

Most visually handicapped children enjoy swimming. Many feel safe and secure in the regular surrounds of a swimming pool. Although most children do not master perfect swimming strokes, they can become fast, competent swimmers able to work side by side with sighted children and also compete against them. Physical education teachers need not fear touching visually handicapped pupils, who will learn quickly if their limbs are put into the correct position or they are allowed to feel the correct position on another person. Provided there is no danger of further damaging their eyes, visually handicapped children can dive into the water to start a race as well as perform standing straight dives from the side of the bath, and dives with tariff difficulty rates from diving boards. Diving has to be closely watched and strict rules must be enforced to avoid the possibility of accidents. Swimming can lead to many other activities. For example, visually

29

handicapped children can take survival and life-saving awards, swim for distance badges and take part in time-trials.

Picture 6. Visually handicapped boys diving in at the start of a race

A swimming pool is a good place in which to introduce canoeing. By using small 'Bat' class canoes, all children can learn sufficient technique to make canoeing on open water much safer. Initially, it is preferable with all beginners to have a one-to-one relationship with the helper. This avoids capsizes in the early stages which can be frightening before children have learnt to balance the canoe. Once this has been achieved, visually handicapped children will progress from hand paddling to using paddles. Totally blind children often find straight paddles easier to use than feathered ones. To keep their hands in the correct position on the shaft, two small strips of raised material can be stuck to the paddle where their hands should grip. All beginners, especially visually handicapped ones, tend to misjudge the side of the bath, so in order to prolong the life of the canoes, it is best to pad the bows with strips of foam rubber. This also protects the bath tiles! It is important that swimming and canoeing do not take place together in a swimming pool as this can lead to serious accidents.

If sailing is part of the school timetable, early capsize practice can be simulated in a swimming bath. Visually handicapped children take longer to grasp quick, vital moves such as those put into action when a dinghy turns over.

Picture 7. One to one help with canoeing

In the warm familiar atmosphere of a pool, while the learning is taking place the whole exercise can become fun. When the children subsequently sail on open water, they will not be so disoriented should their boat capsize. The dinghy used in the practice needs to be small in length without too long a mast. A 'Mirror' dinghy has been used successfully for this practice on many occasions at Dorton House School.

Physical education teachers need not worry over-much about visually handicapped pupils being in more danger than their sighted peers. Generally, it is rare to find blind or partially sighted children who take unnecessary risks, so, provided all the usual safety precautions are taken, 'Let them enjoy the fun' (Scott 1982)

Further reading

Allen, J (1988) 'What is Happening in the Physical Education World?' In: Allen, J. (Ed) (1988) <u>Physical Education. The School Curriculum Development Committee.</u> Department of Education and Science, London : HMSO

Brown, A (1987) 'The Integration of Children with Movement Problems Into the Mainstream Games Curriculum' <u>British Journal of Physical Education,</u> 18, 5, 230-232

Corley, G, Robinson D, Lockett, S (1989) <u>Partially Sighted Children.</u> Windsor : NFER-Nelson

Scott, E P (1982) <u>Your Visually Impaired Student.</u> Baltimore University Press.

4

Outdoor education for visually handicapped children and young people

'Now I know how birds soar and hang gliders fly!!!'

This statement was made by a ten-year-old boy, totally blind from six months of age, whilst standing on a mountain high in the Austrian Alps. He had arrived at this point on the top of the mountain by riding in a chair lift from the village next to the one where he was staying. From the top of the chair lift he had walked with three other young visually handicapped pupils across a four kilometre ridge track. The group were accompanied by a sighted adult. The path was wide and easy but all the children commented on the sound of trickling water and the feel of the mud from the melting snow under their feet. The partially sighted girl was able to see the brightly-coloured Alpine flowers and she described them to the others. The three blind children bent down gently to touch the petals and leaves of the wild crocuses.

Picture 8. Feeling the soft noses and hard horns of the cows.

Lunch was eaten at a remote farmhouse. Close to where the children sat a rich aroma from the cows, still in their winter quarters, wafted over their food.

The children wrinkled their noses at the acrid smell. Seeing their interested faces the farmer led them into the barn, guiding their hands to the soft noses and hard horns of the cows, as shown in picture 8.

Later, as the children made their way down the steep road to the village they walked through newly-cut pine forests. They all remarked on the fresh smell of the pine bark which contrasted with the smell of the cows.

Feeling tired, three of the four rested on a convenient red bench whilst one boy was taken to the opposite side of the road to 'see' and listen to the swish-swish of a scythe cutting the first crop of hay. As he leaned over the edge, a draught of hot air rose from the village some 9800 feet below. As the blast rushed upwards, it caught in his untucked tee shirt and lifted his sun hat high into the air.

   'A thermal!' he exclaimed.

The look of pure joy on his face as understood for the first time what had been keeping the birds in the air and allowed the paragliders he had been told about to float slowly down to the bottom of the mountains, was a delight to watch.

This incident epitomises the challenge and reward that comes from introducing visually handicapped children to outdoor pursuits.

> 'Outdoor education has a unique and invaluable part to play in providing a different, more relevant curriculum, based upon experimental learning, enquiry and problem solving, to enable young people to prepare for the needs of tomorrow.'
> (Keighley, 1985)

Visually handicapped children are as much, if not more so, in need of this approach to learning as sighted children. This point is also emphasised in the DES National Curriculum Proposals for Physical Education (1991). In these proposals outdoor education is considered to be important for the overall development of young people and the important contribution outdoor education makes to the 'social development of pupils' (5.28) is also recognised.

Despite the constrictions of 1265 directed teaching hours and increased pressure on teachers' time, the benefit of introducing outdoor activities to schoolchildren, particularly those with special needs, outweighs these difficulties, especially as it is a requirement of the National Curriculum at all the key stages.

Outdoor education developed from Outward Bound whose founder was Kurt Hahn. He saw the aim of Outward Bound as 'character training through adventure', (Cotton, 1983). The Outward Bound Trust was established in

Aberdovey in 1946. Initially the recipients of these early training courses were young sailors whom it was felt would benefit from a survival course before starting active service. These courses were designed to develop their inner resources through physical as well as mental challenges. The young men attending these 30-day courses benefited from improved self-confidence and a greater understanding of the environment.

Outdoor education is not only about technical instruction needed to take part safely in various activities. Indeed, the shared experience between tutor and students can heighten the awareness and sensitivity of relationships between teachers and the children they teach. Through outdoor activities teachers can become aware, sometimes for the first time, of qualities in children that may not have been obvious in the classroom. This is especially so with the more reserved or shy and with the majority of children with special needs.

Williams (1988) stressed the need to ensure that all children are equipped with some form of physical activity which can become 'part of a future lifestyle'. With the increasing problems of unemployment, visually handicapped children as much, if not more so than others, require 'the skills to keep them fit when utilisation of routine everyday activities is needed'.

Today there is an increasing awareness of the value of outdoor activities for disabled people. At the National Association for Outdoor Education (NADE) Conference in 1986 a statement was made illustrating this.

> 'Outdoor education is committed to active learning through experience, through personal involvement in the wonders and adventures of our environment.' (Moore, 1986)

Activity for handicapped people has come to be increasingly important. The International Year of the Disabled in 1981 made the general public more aware of the needs of disabled people. Handicapped people in society are now no longer content to remain spectators but are actively looking for the opportunity to participate.

> 'The exciting world of outdoor pursuits: not only a feeling of fun, achievement and benefit, but also a realisation that it was not, after all, as difficult or inadvisable as might have been assumed.' (Croucher, 1981)

Outdoor activities for visually handicapped people are regarded as very important for the development of life skills. They open up opportunities for meaningful integration and directly affect attitudes towards a healthy lifestyle. Many visually handicapped pupils have additional emotional problems and outdoor activities can help to overcome these difficulties by providing additional opportunities for expression through movement, increasing belief in themselves and thereby raising their self-esteem. Visually handicapped children can find both pleasure and success by completing a task presented to them through outdoor education and by mastering new techniques.

> 'There is no type of extra-curricular activity, whether it be sailing around the world or going across town to the movies, that cannot be pursued successfully by some visually impaired person.' (Conway et al, 1982)

Outdoor activities provide visually handicapped children with the opportunity for self-discovery, the chance to learn more about themselves and how to accept their own capabilities and limitations. Visually handicapped children often live in closed-in environments: outdoor pursuits are an excellent way of broadening their horizons and teaching them more about the environment and the world they live in.

Mainstream teachers need have no fears about including visually handicapped pupils in outdoor activities. The motivation and enjoyment outdoor pursuits engenders in visually handicapped children is well worth all the extra planning and preparation. Visually handicapped pupils in special schools are often more experienced in outdoor activities such as camping, mountain walking and caving than sighted children. Special schools are often able to offer a much wider range of options in outdoor activities than mainstream schools because they have the time, the good staff/pupil ratios, and also the money. It is essential that integrated visually handicapped children do not miss out on opportunities offered to the rest of the school, simply because of a visual disability. What visually handicapped children can achieve should not be pre-judged because of sighted people's misconceptions. These are often merely the result of not having the opportunity to learn that blindness is a handicap which can be overcome.

Since 1981, the Year of the Disabled, very little research has been done on outdoor activities for handicapped people, especially those who are visually handicapped. It is essential for physical educationists who want to increase their understanding of visually handicapped children and outdoor education to turn towards books and articles written for the sighted and 'acquire a liberal amount of common sense in modifying the content' (Jones, 1984), for children with visual impairments. However, Buell (1983) emphasised that modifying the content of physical activities too much, minimised their value. Although Buell's book remains one of the most informed sources of information on teaching physical education to visually handicapped children, it fails to deal with partially sighted pupils or those being educated outside special schools.

Outdoor activities for visually handicapped children in and around school

The gymnasium, assembly hall, swimming pool and school grounds school are excellent locations for introducing outdoor activities to visually handicapped children. Adventure games, based on outdoor activities, can be created through apparatus imaginatively arranged in the gymnasium. As a continuation of educational gymnastics, visually handicapped children can be introduced to skills such as climbing, swinging, crawling, jumping and balancing. All these skills will come into later use in the mountains, assault courses and activity holidays.

Picture 9. Crawling under a net

Young visually handicapped children are encouraged to strengthen their arms by swinging while holding onto a rope from a gym bench. An added incentive is given if the space between the two benches becomes a 'crocodile pool', or an inclined bench on a wall bar leads them up to a 'secret cave' on the wall ladders that they have to crawl through, and then climb down to fetch a treasure. The list is endless, and all the time these games are played, the children automatically increase body awareness, spatial concepts and team work without realising just how this has been engineered.

Older children can use the apparatus in the gymnasium to improve their fitness and control so that when they reach an assault course, they are strong enough to manage to balance on rope walks, climb over obstacles, swing from trees and slide on aerial runways. Unassisted use of these circuits by totally blind children will be more likely if the same layout of apparatus is used from session to session.

As in educational gymnastics, totally blind pupils will require more assistance to complete these tasks. They will need to be guided over apparatus and led from one activity to another. If the apparatus is left in the same arrangement for several sessions, and pathways are marked with mats and benches, many will be able to cope on their own. Failing this the pupils can work in pairs, a fully sighted child linked with a blind child. If the tasks become too difficult or very high above the ground, there will be times when the teachers themselves will have to guide the visually handicapped pupils until the task has been mastered.

Assault Courses

Assault courses provide a natural, safe extension to work started in the school gymnasium. The children, whatever their eye problem or degree of sight, will find something they can do. It is easy to achieve the thrill of walking on a Bailey rope bridge, or balancing on a log, crawling through a muddy tunnel system or under a net as is clearly illustrated in pictures 9 and 11. Quite naturally, as with all children, there will be certain activities that scare some of them or which they positively dislike. After due encouragement, it is time to move on to the next task. As Croucher said 'Outdoor pursuits should be enjoyed, not suffered'. By stretching a parachute between four trees, the challenge of negotiating the task is quite within the grasp of the totally blind girl in picture 10. The joy on her face is quite obvious.

Picture 10. Stretching a parachute between four trees

It is important for physical educationists to remember that visually handicapped children need to be encouraged verbally. A smile or nod of the head to signify pleasure and success, or raised eyebrows to indicate surprise will suffice with fully sighted children, but not for those with a visual disability.

Picture 11. Crawling through a muddy tunnel system

The assault course specially built by the army for the pupils at Dorton House School for the Blind, was constructed to ensure that from the youngest to the oldest pupils, the least able and the most physically co-ordinated found something to challenge them and in which they could succeed. The pathways between each task are constructed out of soft tree bark chippings, laid down between firm edging boards which differentiate them clearly from the surrounding woodland. This allows the totally blind children to find their own way. They even remark about the 'good scenery' when wriggling through a tight underground squeeze.

There are ridge markers before each new activity, leading them on to the next skill. Visually handicapped children find no difficulty in crawling through dark tunnels, as with caving; they feel secure with confining walls and roof close to them. They are well used to feeling draughts which indicate windows and doorways, and trail their hands to find corners. A tunnel has all these and many more features that can be found on a larger scale in caves.

Orienteering

Orienteering is an excellent outdoor activity for visually handicapped people. Within its controlled rules it provides an experimental opportunity which prepares visually handicapped children and adults with a means to develop emotionally, physically and mentally.

> 'It is a means to an end in which the visually impaired individual gains confidence, skills and concepts that transfer to 'real world' challenges.' (Bina, 1986)

Orienteering is concerned with navigation, making decisions about map reading and interpretation. It improves location awareness and teaches the meaning and method of using and interpreting compasses and compass bearings.

Cotton (1983) illustrated the work of Inge Morisback who used orienteering as a means of teaching visually handicapped people in Norway to increase mobility skills, fitness and tactile sense, when he wrote

> 'Through the combined use of the tactile sense by feeling the map with the hands, the ground with the feet, and the use of the auditive sense by using bearing equipment and listening to nature's own sounds, orienteering is found to be an exciting activity for the blind'.

Visually handicapped children who are introduced to orienteering need to have their courses planned on suitable terrain. This might be local parkland, the school grounds or well known play areas. Orienteering provides an excellent basis for integration. As braille compasses are very basic and directionally limiting, they provide an ideal way to organise team work by linking a braille reader with a partially sighted or sighted partner. The braille reader can have a braille, raised map while his partner works out the direction on an ordinary compass. The Royal School for the Blind in Edinburgh uses thermoform maps. Different ground surfaces are successfully indicated on these raised maps by changing the texture or feel of the plastic. There is no need for complicated courses or difficult map references. A simple orienteering course, successfully completed, can give visually handicapped children a great deal of confidence without too much lengthy preparation. Their ability to learn, to understand and use maps will assist them when they want to start The Duke of Edinburgh Award Scheme.

> 'The most important people in recreation are those who persuade the young to start, to have a go, to try their hand at some sort of sport and physical recreation.' (HRH The Duke of Edinburgh, 1988)

40

Fieldwork studies

Visually handicapped children get a great deal of enjoyment from nature when out walking, but they need specially adapted resources to help them understand what they hear, smell and touch. Fieldwork studies that introduce them to woodland, open downlands, seashore, rivers and ponds widen their understanding of the world they inhabit.

Picture 12. 'Listening' as hands explore the cliff face

Totally blind children will require help to sort out important information about the environment so that they learn to discern the main aspects of what they touch and feel, in contrast to surrounding 'clutter.' Fossils in a cliff face or roots of an upturned tree mean more if the cliff has been explored and the roots of a tree are related to the trunk and the branches. The boy in picture 12 seems to be 'listening' to his hands as they feel the crevices in a chalk cliff at Eastbourne. The same concentration can be seen in picture 13 as these boys learn about tree bark.

Picture 13. Learning about tree bark

Picture 14. Touching the cold torrent from behind a waterfall

Children's ability to differentiate between birds through listening to bird calls can be enhanced if stuffed birds can be felt and scrutinised. Even a partially sighted child has difficulty picking out the similarities and differences between species of birds from visual observation alone. Water is also easy to recognise; if running streams are felt, rivers and lakes are waded through and paddled in, or waterfalls are walked behind. Picture 14 shows visually handicapped children touching the cold torrent from behind a waterfall in the Brecon Beacons.

However environmental and fieldwork studies are introduced to visually handicapped children,

> 'It is doubly important for blind students, whose reasoning powers are so much at the mercy of a reduced and lop-sided sensory intake, that they have as rich a practical experience as possible.' (Hinton, 1984)

Picture 15. Opening the moorland gate

Horse riding

Riding for the disabled has proved to be one of the most therapeutic activities for handicapped children. When on horses, children who have difficulty in getting about are no longer dependent on their own manpower or on mechanical aids. There is a great satisfaction to be gained from sitting on something as strong and powerful as a pony or horse and from learning to control it.

Visually handicapped children, including those with added impairments, both physical and mental, benefit from riding. The company and friendship found

43

from riding the same animal from one lesson to another together with the ease in mobility can make riding the highlight of the week.

The children need to ride under expert guidance. They should be matched to a horse that is suitable for them and work on a one-to-one basis with a helper. The horse must not be too large nor too excitable and needs to accept placidly what is usually orthodox control.

There is nothing to stop a visually handicapped rider from progressing towards independent movement which includes jumping, once the basics have been mastered. Riding has been chosen on many occasions as the option for the Physical Activity Section in the Duke of Edinburgh Award Scheme. The expedition section can also be done on horseback. A teenage boy with advancing Batten's Syndrome, unable to walk for great distances and also totally blind, completed his Bronze Duke of Edinburgh Expedition Section, on horseback, in the Brecon Beacons in Wales. He rode, whilst his other visually handicapped friends walked the distance. Picture 15 shows a visually handicapped rider opening the gate onto moorland.

Cycling

Young visually handicapped children will spend hours cycling tricycles and two-wheelers with stabilisers around familiar play areas.

Cycling is an excellent activity for older visually handicapped pupils. Partially sighted children can ride two-wheelers around the school grounds or other quiet roads and tracks. Totally blind children can ride tandems with a fully sighted person. Many local cycling clubs possess tandem bikes and members are more than willing to take blind children for rides. Cycling is good for general fitness and team work. The benefits from cycling, as part of a fitness programme, can equally be gained from using fixed exercise bikes. The advantage of cycling outside is that environments can change. There are now tandem mountain bikes, so the opportunities for introducing visually handicapped children to rough tracks and hills are endless.

Roller skating

Roller skating is another popular activity with visually handicapped children. They learn to balance on skates in exactly the same way as sighted children do. Once the skill has been mastered, they are able to skate on paths and hard areas around school or home. It is essential that a blind roller skater is closely watched or alternatively uses the area on his or her own, to avoid collisions with others.

A closed-in, hard area, such as a court or football pitch, also makes an excellent roller skating space. Totally blind children need to learn how to use echo rebounds from the sides to avoid crashing into them. This might be a clicking noise from their mouths, clicking fingers and thumbs or clapping hands. Once learnt, this technique can give them remarkable freedom.

All children should wear protective knee and elbow pads and hard helmets when roller skating. Visually handicapped children need to avoid any further damage to their eyesight, and a hard helmet will help to ensure this.

Campcraft

Most schools have some grass areas where tents can be erected. Visually handicapped children are quite capable of putting up their own tents. At first, they need guidance until they can discern the difference between poles, ropes and pegs. Practising putting up tents while at school saves time when the children are away on camps. This is illustrated in picture 16. Campcraft is another activity that visually handicapped children can master whilst the others in the group are playing field games. Other sighted pupils can learn how to help visually handicapped friends without doing the task for them.

Picture 16. Practising putting up tents while at school

Camping is an excellent activity for integrating visually handicapped pupils. Again, if they have rehearsed putting up tents and cooking before they go away, they will be able to take a positive, active part in the trip and not wait passively for the end result. The line drawings illustrate how visually handicapped children can learn to become competent at putting up tents.

Campcraft

Picture 17. Finding the 'A' piece   Picture 18. It's easy when you know how

Picture 19. Not all tents are the same shape   Picture 20. Pegs

Outdoor activities outside school

Water based activities

The options for water based activities for visually handicapped people are extensive. Knowledge of how to swim and having confidence in the water are very important. Even severely handicapped children can take part in water sports provided they do not have a fear of getting wet and being submerged occasionally. Preferably, of course, they should learn how to swim.

Canoeing

Once pupils have learnt the basic skills necessary for canoeing, that is balancing, paddling and getting in and out safely, canoeing on rivers and lakes becomes exciting and rewarding. Occasionally, still water in lakes and rivers can become rough, so it is important for visually handicapped children to have experienced the sensation of turbulence by teachers simulating waves in a pool. With canoe spray decks on, (aprons that keep out the water as seen in picture 21), the children hold the sides of a canoe while the helper bounces up and down on the stern. With several canoes at once doing this, a swimming pool can become as rough as wild water, a situation illustrated in picture 22.

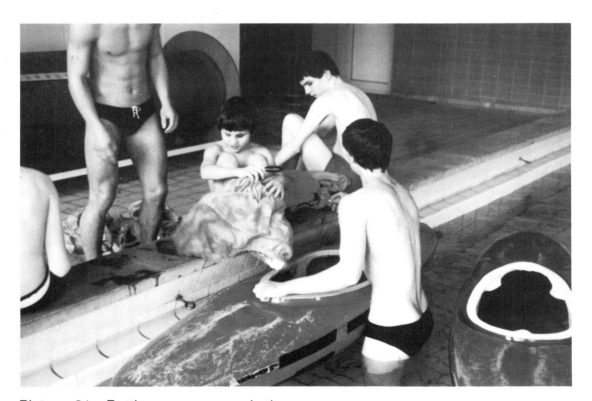

Picture 21. Putting on a spray deck

Canoe edges need to be smooth, as it is very uncomfortable for pupils to graze or cut themselves on a canoe cockpit when getting into it. Visually handicapped children can easily hurt themselves as they are unable to see jagged edges.

Picture 22. Waves

Visually handicapped children enjoy paddling Canadian canoes. This way, sighted helpers can work alongside them. Others who are more experienced can canoe on their own, moving towards sound cues, or following a guide who talks to them. Guiding is more comfortable from behind the visually handicapped canoeist, and it saves having a constant crick in the neck. On open water the smell of the water, sounds from the shore and from across the river or lake, give visually handicapped children a sense of space and freedom.

Despite being totally blind, it is possible for children to feel confident in a canoe and to master the technique of feathering the paddle.

In picture 23, visually handicapped canoeists are waiting to backpaddle in a race against other canoeists. This is a good example of how sighted and non-sighted children can work together. Picture 24 shows the technique of rafting canoes together, another example of integrating the visually handicapped children with sighted guides.

Picture 23. Preparing to backpaddle

Games can be played when canoes are rafted together. As soon as everyone is firmly holding on to the adjacent canoe on each side, one child can climb out carefully from his or her cockpit and, with help, walk across the canoe bridge.

Picture 24. Canoes rafted together

Rowing

Rowing is another water based activity that can be great fun. It is excellent for integration and, as with sailing, it is better to have a sighted crew member working with a visually handicapped child. Once the layout of the boat has been understood, the technique of rowing can be easily developed.

Sailing

It is important that visually handicapped children are taught to sail by instructors who understand their emotional, physical, mental and medical needs. Sailing is a sport that has gained in popularity over the last 20 to 30 years. If there is not a qualified sailing instructor on the school staff, local clubs should be approached. Many sailors who work for the first time with visually handicapped children are amazed at their ability to pick up the basic skills.

It is vital to spend time allowing children to feel the boat, the mast, the sheets and tackle and the rudder before they start on the water. This can be seen in picture 25. Capsize can be practised in a swimming pool, but it is important to put all children through a capsize drill in open water as soon as they start sailing. This takes away the fear of turning over. Instructors obviously take great care not to put out in very strong winds when the children are learning. To minimise the chance of any sailing dinghy inverting, an empty plastic two-gallon bottle can be tied to the mast. Should the boat capsize, it will not then 'turn turtle.'

Picture 25. Getting to know the boat

Visually handicapped children always need a fully sighted person in the boat with them as either the crew or helm. They learn to sail by feeling the wind on their faces, sensing the keel of the boat and listening to the noise the sails make. All sailors 'feel' their boats, especially when trimming them closely.

Navigation requires sight, particularly in crowded water, but visually handicapped children can learn to crew and helm boats. On sea-going craft, an audible compass can be installed. When set, it remains silent. If the course is lost, however, the compass immediately begins to bleep, one signal for port, the other for starboard. The visually handicapped helmsman then moves the rudder or steering wheel accordingly. Helming a large boat is great fun as picture 26 shows.

Sailing can allow handicapped children to move at speed for the first time in their lives. On the BBC television programme 'Go For It', a boy sailing on a river estuary said that he had never felt so proud in his life. Instead of arriving last at every occasion, he came first!

The Jubilee Sailing Trust gives disabled people an opportunity to work at sea as crew members on an ocean-going square-rigger ship, 'The Lord Nelson'. On the one-week voyages handicapped people are linked to the able-bodied. Metal arrows are used to give blind crew members directions round the decks, the sharp end always pointing towards the bows. The object of the Trust is

> 'to have everybody working together doing whatever they're
> able to do at the speed of the slowest person on board.'

('Wish You Were Here', Independent Television, 1981)

In 1981, with a sighted crew, a blind boy from Dorton House School helmed a 'Miracle' Dinghy, presented to the school by Richard Stilgoe of the BBC's 'Nationwide' programme in the National Championships. He has now left school, but owns his own boat and sails regularly at this local sailing club. He and his sighted crew have won several events. Introduction to sailing at school gave him a lifetime physical activity to pursue.

Picture 26. Helming a large boat is great fun

Hay Rafting

Hay rafting was introduced to the children at Dorton House School by Dick Boetius. Since 1975 Dick has given hours of his time teaching visually handicapped children field studies and mountain activities.

Initially a large tarpaulin is laid on the ground and hay or straw is piled onto it. When full, the edges are gathered up and laced tightly together. Before the end flaps are secured, several boards are laid down which provide a platform to sit on. Once on the water, a hay raft will remain afloat for hours. It can be paddled about or towed behind a motor boat.

Picture 27. Laying the tarpaulin on the ground

Picture 28. Gathering the hay

Picture 29. Bringing the edges of the tarpaulin together

Picture 30. Securing the flaps

53

Visually handicapped children have for many years, enjoyed the fun of making hay rafts and felt very pleased with themselves when they have launched them. Provided the platform is firm, less able students can be secure on a hay raft as easily as the able bodied. Sighted guides should be used at all times either on the raft or close by. Hay rafts would make Arthur Ransome proud!

Picture 31. Launching the hay raft

Safety

Whatever the water activity, suitable clothing and buoyancy aids must always be worn.

Mountain Activities

Mountains provide a challenge to people from all walks of life.

Outdoor pursuits can make the difference between inactivity in later life and one extended by a variety of experiences. Visually handicapped children who are fortunate enough to be introduced to mountain activities while they are at school, very often develop a life-long interest in them. These may be camping, hill walking, rock climbing, skiing or caving. Combinations and permutations of these and others both in summer and winter, provide excitement and challenge that test both visually handicapped and sighted children alike.

Mountaineering

Living and moving in mountainous regions gives visually handicapped children the chance to succeed, whatever their level of ability. In the mountains every precaution needs to be taken to ensure the safety of everyone in the group. The mountain code must be followed and the group led by a fully qualified instructor who has British Mountain Association (BMA) training plus experience with visually handicapped children. When mountain walking with visually handicapped children, more local sighted help is needed in difficult terrain. A totally blind child needs to walk one-to-one with a fully sighted, competent guide.

Leading visually handicapped children over mountains is not difficult. Experience helps, but the necessary technique can easily be learnt. The method of guiding children varies with the individual. Some prefer to tuck an arm inside that of the guide. Others have their wrist held. On easy terrain it is possible to walk beside a sighted guide and keep in touch shoulder to shoulder. Younger children prefer a firm grip. The guide needs to watch the ground carefully, and prepare the visually handicapped person before an obstacle is reached. This way the rhythm of the walk can be kept going, making it far less tiring for both the blind person and the sighted guide. Picture 32 shows a sighted helper leading a blind girl. The helper can be seen looking carefully at his feet in order to guide her smoothly over rough ground.

Picture 32. Walking and talking brings the environment to life

A totally blind 11 year old, climbing in Austria explained

> 'We learnt if you climb mountains you can't just put one foot in front of the other, you have to put your foot down slowly, take the weight on that foot before you attempt to put the weight on the other one.'

In the mountains time needs to be taken to feel the rocks, trees, grasses and flowers. The girl in picture 33 is reading the gravestone of five year old Tommy Jones who died on the top of the Brecon Beacons. It is important to remember that the exhilaration of seeing mountain peaks is lost to visually handicapped people. Putting one foot in front of another for hours without descriptions being given, can be anything but enlightening. Leading a visually handicapped child over mountains requires care and an imaginative interpretation of what sighted people take for granted.

Picture 33. Reading the gravestone of Tommy Jones on Brecon Beacons

When walking in mountains, it is useful to have a ski pole in the free hand. This acts as a stick and a prop and is especially useful on steep, narrow or icy ground. Walking in winter or in high glacier regions is quite possible.

On ice, when crampons are needed, it is essential to lead a visually handicapped person who is using the old type of crampon, which do not have front spikes. Modern crampons' forward spikes can rip open the leg and heel of a sighted guide. A successful method of attaching a blind child to a sighted guide on steep and narrow paths is by a central crab on the leader's back. The blind child wears a belt, with a crab that can swivel from the front to the back. The visually handicapped child is then able to walk directly in the footsteps of the sighted guide. Examples of this technique are illustrated in Chapter 5, in a description of the 1981 Expedition to the Pyrenees.

Young children who lack adult strength enjoy stopping to listen and feel. The expedition to Austria described in Chapter 5, illustrates the wide experience that a week in the mountains can give visually handicapped children of junior school age, especially if they are integrated with sighted friends.

Camping

Camping in the wild is beneficial for all children. Putting up tents and sleeping at night with the sounds of wind in the trees, water, night-time

Picture 34. Team work in gathering wood

animals and birds, fascinates visually handicapped children. All tents have smells and the light changes to being orange or green through the canvas. The sound of rain on the tight tent walls is invigorating and the whole experience is very different from the visually handicapped children's normal sleeping arrangements.

They can also take part in the day-to-day running of a camp, for instance collecting wood, fetching water, helping to prepare food and cooking it or washing up. Less able visually handicapped children can be seen working as a team gathering wood in picture 34. Visual problems must not be used as an excuse to get out of the menial chores of camping.

The friendships made during a camp can last for a long time. Visually handicapped children who are often musically gifted can come into their own around a camp fire by leading the singing and providing the music.

Rock Climbing

The challenge of mastering a rock climb is exhilarating. Rock climbing is an ideal activity for visually handicapped people because it is a contact sport, providing a physical and mental challenge, and requiring strength and a good sense of touch. Climbing is non-competitive and therefore it is ideal for less able children who can succeed on their own merit. It is an activity that once learnt, can easily be continued after school.

As Tullis (1986) wrote 'Getting off the ground is often the hardest part'. Once a blind or partially sighted child is on the rock, it is important to build up confidence. Whilst climbing, it is essential to talk through each move. For example:

> 'There's a pocket hold at two o'clock, put your fingers in and pull to the left.'

> 'A ledge is just above your waist, press down with both your hands and walk your feet up.' (Ibid)

Julie Tullis, the British mountaineer who died on K2 in the Himalayas in 1986, used to progress from talking blind children up rock climbs to tapping the rock where the next hold was as seen in picture 35. She noticed that partially sighted children often had greater difficulty in climbing than blind children because of their distorted view of the next holds.

When climbing, all children need to be correctly dressed in suitable clothes and footwear. Visually handicapped children will tend to bang their knees and elbows, therefore long trousers and sleeves are essential. Helmets must be worn and correct harnesses and belts used. **No climbing must be attempted without fully qualified instructors.** Where there are no such instructors on the school staff, children could attend a centre such as Bowles, near Tunbridge Wells, or Harrison's Rocks at Groombridge in Kent. Similar centres can be found throughout the country, where children whatever their ability or disability, will learn under expert guidance. It is

Picture 35. Looking for the next hold

important to remember that once a visually handicapped child has reached the top of the climb, observation from the staff must not become lax. In the exuberance of the climb visually handicapped children can forget about their location and step back off the rock once they have been unclipped from the safety harness. They need to be guided carefully down to the bottom before anyone relaxes.

The following description of a day spent climbing Harrison's Rocks, was written by a blind 15 year old girl:

> 'We did not know what to expect when we set out for
> Harrison's Rocks. We were very surprised by the way the
> rocks were set out. Climbing the rocks themselves was a
> totally different experience. We found it very interesting, the
> different abilities each rock required.
>
> Being blind, when it came to climbing the rocks we found the
> height of them very daunting, especially when you could not
> find a hand hold. Even though we could not see the height it

59

was frightening when you could hear people's voices down below, you realised how high up you were.

We found it a very interesting but tiring experience. We were prepared for it to be hard but we did not expect it to be quite so physical. However, it was a thoroughly enjoyable experience.'

Caving

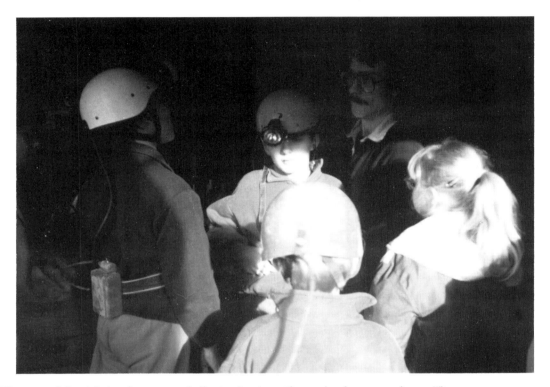

Picture 36. Listening carefully to instructions before caving

Caving is an ideal activity for visually handicapped people, providing adventure and comradeship in exciting environments. Visually handicapped children are fascinated by the contrast in the feel of different textures of rock and mud. Directions can be worked out by listening to the flow of underground water. Children can 'feel their world around them' as they crawl through tunnels and crouch under low overhangs. It can be most rewarding for the instructor to observe children's reactions when for the first time they experience what Penman (1970) calls

'the beauty of the under-world, the eeriness of a dark swirling river, or the excitement of climbing down a swinging ladder.'

Suitable clothing must be worn. Caves remain at a constant temperature, and feet and bodies frequently become wet. Unless children are swimming underground or going through sump holes, they do not need wet suits. Led by an experienced, qualified instructor, children can wear old track suits or boiler suits, wellingtons and helmets. While totally blind children do not need lights and heavy battery cells, partially sighted children do. With all children and especially those who are caving for the first time, it is important to keep in mind the level of excitement and stress that an activity such as caving can give.

Picture 37. A totally blind girl entering a narrow and dark mine

The children at Dorton House School are introduced to caving in the old mines at Merstham. They wear exactly the same equipment as they do in caving, and the feeling of being underground is just as exciting. Here, there is very little water except by the entrances, so they do not get too wet. The mines have several entrances, some of which are via plastic tubes. These do not worry totally blind children as seen in picture 37.

Feeling the roughly-hewn sides of the tunnels and very lightly touching the stalactites and stalagmites is educational as well as physically challenging. These mines were excavated between 17th and 19th centuries to provide stone to rebuild central London after the Great Fire of 1666. During the early 20th century they were used by mushroom growers. Now they are the property of the Croydon Caving Club.

Skiing

'If a physically inactive blind person can suddenly conquer something so outlandish as skiiing, a sport that challenges even the sighted, then he will know that there is no limit to what can be achieved.' (O'Rear and O'Rear, 1976)

Picture 38. A five year old on the dry ski slope at Dorton House School

It is important to observe a visually handicapped child skiing to understand fully the enjoyment and exhilaration skiing can give blind people. Visually handicapped children learn to ski in exactly the same way as sighted children. Careful instruction is needed to build up their confidence and to enable them to master the basic skills. Plastic slopes are an ideal starting place. (Picture 38) Totally blind children tend to crouch too low when they ski. Unable to observe better skiers and learn from them, they feel more secure bending over their ski tips, often with their bottoms stuck out. Patient coaching can overcome this.

Picture 39. The crouching stance and an instructor skiing backwards

Blind skiers can learn more easily from a one-to-one relationship with their instructor. Often an instructor will ski backwards down the mountain in front of a visually handicapped child, talking and coaching. This way, the instructor can stop the child if he or she loses control. Crouching stance and instruction can be seen in picture 39. Alternatively, poles can be used. A long one, with the instructor in the middle can allow two children to ski under his guidance at one time. Ski sticks held parallel to the ground can allow visually handicapped children freedom of movement the first time they ski. Fixing their skis in a small snowplough position, the instructor can ski down the mountain with the children matching his every move. This builds up their confidence very quickly.

Use of ski lifts can cause some problems with visually handicapped children. Rope drag lifts are easy to use, provided the children know when to let go. Button lifts are possible, once a blind child can ski, if someone is waiting to meet them at the end of the lift. Double 'T' bar lifts are easy once the technique of staying up and allowing the lift to do the work is learnt. A visually handicapped child can use a 'T' bar lift with a sighted person as guide. Should children find any of these techniques too difficult to master at first, they can use them with an adult directly behind, who takes them up between their knees. Chair lift operators need to be told if the children are visually handicapped. On a single lift, provided somebody is at the top to help children off, a blind child who has experience of using these lifts can cope. A double lift is preferable, as a sighted person can help to lift the bar at the correct time.

If blind or handicapped people are using chair lifts or gondolas, the operators will warn the men at the top that they are on their way, and place a distinctive marker on the back or side of their chair or bubble. This will ensure that the chair lift is slowed down to give more time for a visually impaired person to get off. Knowing this will help stem any fears ski group organisers might have of taking visually handicapped children to the high slopes.

Once the children can ski well, distinctive marker bibs should be worn by both the blind skier and the sighted guide. In this way, the two skiers can ski down the slopes and others will keep out of their way. The guide calls the skier from in front, telling him when to turn right or left, and where there are steeper parts of patches of ice. For a totally blind skier the slopes should not be too bumpy, rocky or extensively covered in ice. Never on any account should a severely partially sighted or totally blind child be allowed to ski alone. This is dangerous for the visually impaired skier and for any adult or child with whom they might collide.

A great deal is known about the dangers of mountains, but skiing for the visually handicapped need cause no more worries than with sighted children. Skiing has to be well planned, the ski school advised in advance if blind skiers are going to join a sighted party, or if personal guides are to be provided for each visually handicapped party member. These guides must be experienced skiers who have additional qualifications. Advice on how to obtain qualifications as a visually impaired ski leader can be given by the British Ski Club for the Disabled whose address appears in Appendix 2.

Cross country skiing is an excellent activity for visually handicapped people and this type of skiing can be performed anywhere where it is flat and there is sufficient snow. The equipment is less expensive than for alpine skiing. Cross country skiing is an excellent way of getting fit. A blind skier can fit skis into the track of a sighted guide, and away they go! Cross country skiing opens up mountain tracks to visually handicapped people that would be impassable on foot in the winter. Alternatively, flat tracks laid out on fields or roads are equally good. As Pitzer (1984) said

'All you need is a little snow'

Other activities visually handicapped children might enjoy

Shooting

The sound of pellets hitting a target of tin cans and plates is amusing and exciting for visually handicapped children. Under expert guidance, visually handicapped children can learn to fire air rifles and pistols. Precision shooting is very difficult to master, since it requires sound cues and audio sightings, but hearing pellets bounce off random targets can give visually handicapped children hours of pleasure.

Ice skating

With the help of a sighted guide, visually handicapped children can learn to skate well. They have no more difficulty learning to balance on ice skates than anyone else, and this sport can provide enjoyment throughout adult life. Skating requires a developed sense of touch and provided visually impaired skaters are guided around the rink they will find that this will assist their technique.

Golf

Golf is becoming an increasingly popular sport for visually handicapped people. It is an excellent activity for promoting integration, as a blind golfer needs a sighted companion or caddy to guide him or her through the course and to find the balls.

Golf for visually handicapped people was started in the UK in 1982 and is now well established throughout the world. Although a difficult sport to master for blind as well as for sighted people, golf is quite within the capacity of blind people, and when mastered can give a great feeling of satisfaction, (Benwell, 1991). Golf is increasingly taught in special schools for the visually impaired. School staff in mainstream schools could include golf as an option for visually handicapped pupils. Further details of how to play and how to coach golf can be found in the information section at the end of the book.

Archery

Archery for visually handicapped people is an advanced sport. Children shooting arrows at targets covered in balloons get an idea of whether they have aimed correctly or not. With help, the boy in picture 40 will know immediately he is on target. Partially sighted children will be able to see a brightly-coloured board.

Picture 40. Archery

Conclusion

'Spending leisure time in self-fulfilling recreation activities is essential to visually handicapped individuals' well-being. Visually handicapped individuals have a right to learn what options are available. Whether they decide to use their leisure time reading a novel off the best seller list, going fishing, gambling, or mountain climbing is unimportant.' (Huebner, 1986)

If visually handicapped schoolchildren, whether in special or mainstream education have the opportunity to choose sporting and recreational activities, they will be able to achieve far more than if they sit around for the rest of their lives. Dave Hurst is an example of a physically motivated blind man. He lost his sight some years ago but was determined to remain mobile. At the time of writing, Dave is in the National Judo Squad, water skis and climbs.

Very few visually handicapped children will be as motivated or as able as Dave Hurst, but if they have been given the chance to experience a variety of activities, they will at least have the opportunities to try.

There is always a danger that eager people will take visually handicapped children out on trips to mountains, parks, forests, rivers and lakes and put them into situations which are not pleasurable to them. It is always vital to remember that there is a difference between taking part in an activity to widen visually handicapped children's experience and the guides doing these to enhance their own esteem. The tutor's enthusiasm must not overshadow the personal likes and dislikes of the children.

Further reading

Benwell, D (1991) 'Golf: What's your handicap?' New Beacon LXXV, 891, 389-391

Bina, M J (1986) 'Orienteering : Activities Leading to Skills Development' Journal of Visual Impairment and Blindness, 80, 5, 735-739

Buell, C E (1983) Physical Education for Blind Children Illinois : Charles Thomas

Care, C (1988) 'The Changing Face of Outdoor Education' British Journal of Physical Education, 19, 2, 52-54

Croucher, N (1981) Outdoor Pursuits for Disabled People London : Woodhead - Faulkner Ltd

DES (1991) National Curriculum Proposals for PE London : HMSO

Eaves, M (1988) 'The National Advice and Information Centre for Outdoor Education : a resource for all' British Journal of Physical Education, 19, 2, 55-57

Fox, K (1988) 'The Child's Perspective in Physical Education Part 5 : The Self-Esteem Complex' British Journal of Physical Education, 19, 6, 247-252

Fox, K (1988) 'The Child's Perspective in Physical Education Part 5 : The Self-Esteem Complex' British Journal of Physical Education, 19, 6, 247-252

Hinton, R (1984) 'Ecological Fieldwork with Visually Handicapped Students' British Journal of Visual Impairment, 11, 2, 41-44

Huebner, K M (1986) 'Social Skills' In : Scholl, G T (Ed) Foundations of Education for Blind and Visually Handicapped Children and Youth New York : American Foundation for the Blind

Independent Television, 'Wish You Were Here' No. 14 (ITV) (1989)

Jones, G (1984) 'Review of Buell' (1983) Physical Education for Blind Children' British Journal of Visual Impairment, 1, 2, 57-58

Keighley, P (1985) 'Using the Potential of Outdoor Education as a Vehicle for Integrated Learning' Adventure Education, 2, 4/5, 26-30

Moore, I (1986) 'The Games We Play' Adventure Education, 1, 6, 18-19

O'Rear, J and O'Rear, F (1976) 'I can do anything' Readers Digest, November 1976.

Penman, E (1970) 'Caving' In : Parker, T (Ed) (1970) An Approach to Outdoor activities. London : Pelham Books

Pitzer, J R (1974) 'Nordic Ski Touring for the Visually Handicapped' Education of the Visually Handicapped, IV, 2, 63-64

Standevan, J (1987) 'Education for Leisure' British Journal of Physical Education, 18, 2, 77-78

Tullis, J (1986) Clouds From Both Sides. London : Grafton (1986)

Warren, D H (1984) Blindness and early Childhood Development, 2nd Edition, Revised. New York : American Foundation for the Blind

Williams, A (1988) 'Physical Activity Patterns Among Adolescents - Some Curriculum Implications' Physical Education Review, 11, 1, 28-39

5

Expeditions with visually handicapped children

All children benefit from the chance to take part in an expedition into unknown territory at least once during their schooldays. Expeditions provide a means of integrating sighted and visually handicapped children in a meaningful way where each can play a positive part in the activity. Expeditions also provide the opportunity to use many skills previously learnt in physical education at school. Agility, determination, fitness, sharing, overcoming fear of the unknown, and much more, naturally occur during an expedition.

Through organising expeditions my experience has proved time and time again that on most occasions it is the sighted guides who gain as much from a mixed group as the visually handicapped members. Knowing that another person is trusting and relying on you gives many sighted helpers a feeling of well being. Careful preparation and meticulous planning by the leaders will usually ensure the creation of a united integrated group. The sighted pupils lead the way and the visually impaired children enhance the experience by using their ears and moving in harmony with their sighted partners.

The following examples of expeditions into the mountains of France and Austria illustrate the value of including visually handicapped children in outdoor activities. Mainstream teachers need not fear that blind and partially sighted children have to be barred from the outdoor activities requirement of the National Curriculum.

Safety of paramount importance at all times. Throughout this chapter reference is made to safety and the importance of showing each member of a group how to respond to hazards and avoid danger.

Expeditions with visually handicapped children

Expeditions offer visually handicapped children ' the potential for embarking on a vehicle of self-discovery, a journey without end' (Percy 1989). These expeditions require as much, if not more, planning than do those for sighted children. The most important thing to remember is that more help is needed.

In a sighted group, one or two visually handicapped pupils can easily be incorporated into expeditions without too much difficulty. All the helpers need training and reassurance that the task is not beyond them. It is unrealistic to expect anyone, however well qualified they are in their own field, to lead a blind or severely partially sighted child over rough ground, up rock faces, across lakes or underground without first having had demonstrated to them methods of guiding. Guiding a visually handicapped child requires both physical and verbal contact. Sighted guides have to learn to verbalise their instructions. They need to feel confident, and at ease with the task at hand in order to make the experience of leading visually handicapped children worthwhile and enjoyable. The physical and verbal contact between sighted and visually handicapped people when they are moving together encourages trust and friendship. Language is important as it brings to life the environment, making expeditions enjoyable for everyone.

1981 - International Year of the Disabled
Expedition to the ice-caves in the Pyrenees

In 1981 five senior boys from Dorton House School for the Blind, under the leadership of Dick Boetius, climbed 9,000 feet to the 'Grotte de Catenet' an ice cave high in the French Pyrenees. In addition to the five boys, three of whom were totally blind the party included five fully sighted guides. The group drove from Sevenoaks to France and established base at camp Gavrance, 6,000 feet up in the Pyrenees.

Putting up large tents at altitude in strong winds takes time and effort. It is quite possible for the totally blind pupils in the group to anchor the tent poles while others start to peg the sides down. Putting up a tent is a team effort.

To acclimatise the boys and to give them experience of walking over difficult rock at altitude, the first day was spent around the camp. All the boys had experience of hill walking in Wales, but none had moved at this altitude. Without packs, the boys and their guides were able to experiment with different methods of leading, and get to know and understand each other.

The following day, carrying 30 lb packs or more, the party set off to climb towards their altitude camp at the 'Brete de Roland,' a window in the rock, 10,000 feet above them. Before the ground became more arduous the visually impaired members of the party were led by holding lightly onto the arm of their sighted guide. Picture 41 illustrates this. It clearly shows the sighted guide walking half a step in front of his blind partner. This allows him to place his own feet first and then be followed by the blind climber. This method of leading allows the sighted guide to use his eyes to select the best footholds and in addition to describing verbally what is next, he can easily change direction. If the blind person walks to the side of a guide on difficult terrain guiding becomes much harder as the sighted guide has to simultaneously watch where his own feet are to be placed as well as his partner's. This becomes very tiring in a short time and leads to stumbling which will in turn result in falls.

As a mountain guide it is important to know how to describe footholds to a visually impaired person. It is no good giving them the description after they have taken the step. If footholds are talked about in the future tense as the guide makes the move, the blind climber will know what is in front of him. This technique comes with practice but an experienced visually impaired mountain walker will very soon know if he is with a knowledgeable guide.

Party leaders must explain to the sighted team members well in advance what their role is. This will ensure that a long, difficult climb will be carried out safely in a relaxed way. After a long walk or climb the test is passed if both the sighted and visually impaired team members want to carry on.

It was not long before the rock gave way to snow and ice coverage. In 1981, the party carried ice axes which acted as stabilisers and probes on the ice and snow. Today, ski poles would be used and on ice, crampons are required. With help, a visually handicapped boy can attach his own crampons. Using his hands to feel the straps, he can align the spikes in the correct place. The students in the party who were blind used 10 point 'scissor' crampons to avoid damaging their guide's Achilles tendons.

Picture 41. Setting off across the mountain, carrying 30lb packs

Ten point crampons do not have the two forward spikes that are fitted to the modern 12 point crampons.

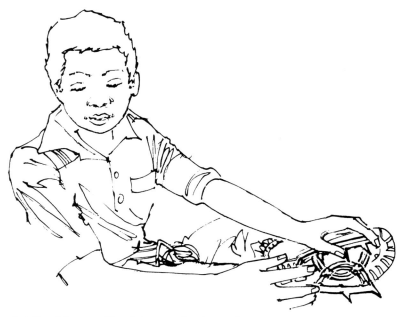

Picture 42. A blind boy attaching a 'scissor' crampon

Leading a visually handicapped person on snow and ice requires careful consideration. When moving over narrow, steep gradients it is essential to have them directly behind the leader. This is possible if they are led with a sling attached to a 'D' ring on the guide's belt. The blind walker can then place his hand along the sling to hold onto the middle of the guide's back, ensuring that he will follow directly in the guide's path.

Picture 43. Attached to a sling and a 'D' ring to a sighted guide

When the ascent became steep, it was found preferable to rope a sighted guide to a visually handicapped walker on a one-to-one basis. Normally the whole party would be roped together, but in this case if a visually handicapped walker takes a wrong step, he can drag the rest of the party down with him. This can be dangerous on narrow, steep ridges that drop sharply away on one side. It is at these times that an ice axe or ski pole is very important for both the guide and the visually handicapped walker.

Picture 44. Climbing a steep ascent on a one to one basis

Similarly, when traversing narrow inclines, both the guide and his visually handicapped partner need to be attached to a guide rope. Movement must be slow and careful, the guide taking his blind partner through each move.

The expedition in 1981 came to its climax when the ice caves were reached. Moving in away from the hot sun to feel the sheet ice descending from the roof required the pupils to take great care as well as to have extra clothing.

A visual handicap does not deter anyone from enjoying the exhilaration and challenge of mountains, both at home and abroad. Under expert guidance a party such as this can move easily over difficult ground and achieve the same destinations as a party of sighted people.

Austria 1988 - 1989
'Walking inside a cloud'

What is a cloud to a congenitally totally blind child - a white or grey mass of cotton wool in the sky? Cotton wool is dense, clouds are not. But the air turbulence that leads to the formation of clouds can make even a large aeroplane drop and wobble, and tummies feel 'left behind.' But this has still not explained what a cloud is to someone who has never seen one.

In 1988 whilst I was walking at a height of 6,500 ft in Austria with a group of visually handicapped 10 year olds, the weather suddenly closed in. Bright sunlight vanished as a storm whipped up. The light rapidly disappeared and rain came in at right angles. 'The atmosphere is different' said a totally blind child holding onto my right arm. 'Are we inside a cloud?'

Yes, we were. It was cold and very wet, thunder rumbled in the distance and walking became increasingly difficult. Now these children knew what a rain-cloud 'felt' like. They put out hands to feel it, but only the rain touched their palms. 'The atmosphere feels heavier' they said. The rain and wind certainly added to this sensation.

June 1988

In June 1988 four visually handicapped pupils from the Junior School at Dorton House had the opportunity to stay for a week in the Austrian Tyrol. The Keller family, who own the Kellerwirt Hotel in Oberau, invited the author to take the children to stay as their guests.

Oberau is a village in the Wildschonau Valley which translates as 'wild and beautiful.' Wildschonau is a valley that lives up to its name. The wild, wooded mountains rise steeply on either side of the valley, giving endless opportunities for mountain walking along well-marked paths.

Three of the children were totally blind while the fourth had a useful amount of vision. During the week the children spent over 30 hours in the mountains, experiencing paths, rocks, deep forests and high ridges during their excursions. Without exception, they all negotiated the natural obstacles, absorbing the atmosphere with intelligent interest. They noticed the different bird calls, the hums of the insects, the whirs of the grasshoppers and the sounds of rushing torrents. The totally blind children remarked on the hard effort and time it took to walk to the top of a 6,500 foot peak, but were rewarded when they felt the roughness of the wooden cross that marked the summit.

Their first attempt at scrambling over rocks was accepted without fear. All the visually handicapped children I have ever taken to rocks have remarked on the many different textures they have felt with their hands. The rocks on the Wildschonau are granite and limestone. There were plenty of opportunities for feeling scree under their boots. One child remarked on the similarity of the sound of his feet sliding over the loose stones and the sound of water running over rocks in a stream. Even through the thick soles of their mountain boots, they were well aware of the difference between rocks and tree roots. On the whole the children preferred the rough,

74

bumpy, rocky surfaces. They also noticed and enjoyed the experience of walking across snow pockets where the crust broke as they walked.

Throughout the week, the children all matured. They became fitter and leaner, enjoying three good meals a day. One boy, who made the most progress, became absorbed with the sounds of bird song and in collecting snails and slugs from the surrounding walls of the swimming pool. He was able to hold many intelligent conversations with us and other adults staying in the hotel, whereas at school he was thought to be deeply disturbed and in need of psychiatric help.

When not walking in the mountains the children swam, rode horses, joined the village band and met many of the local people. The whole week was an undoubted success, so much so that the group was invited to return the following year.

June 1989

The planning needed for any outdoor activity trip is long and intricate. Now that public notice has been drawn so tragically to the dangers involved in taking children to the mountains, staff have to be even more vigilant. With visually handicapped children it is essential to ensure that all possible eventualities are covered. Mainly, this means the extra support that is required both out on the hills and in the hotel or base where the children are staying. With visually handicapped children of junior age, a trip such as this to Austria may well be the first time they have been away from home, other than living as weekly boarders in school.

From the moment the party left the familiar surroundings of school early one Friday morning, the feeling of the group was one of excited expectancy. Three children had been to Austria before but one was flying for the very first time.

Without doubt the benefit of taking a group of junior children on trips like this is that they become sufficiently motivated to ensure that they have a long and lasting interest in mountain walking. Living amongst village people, meeting other guests in the hotel, choosing their food, and showering alone, are at once major differences from closely supervised lives at home and school. Some require more help than others, yet it is team work that shines through. Walking around the building, grounds and down the village street becomes a challenge that, once overcome, produces a feeling of instant success. If an activity that boosts self-confidence is needed, living in a small, friendly community, sharing experiences with strangers and mastering feelings of tiredness, mountains must come high on the list of suitable options.

Staying at the same hotel this year were an elderly couple who were in their late seventies. Both the husband and his wife were rapidly losing their sight with glaucoma. Meeting four visually handicapped children who spoke quite naturally of the 'feelings' and 'frustrations' of blindness, both surprised and enlightened them. The couple very much wanted to reach the top of a mountain. It seemed a natural thing to include them on a gondola trip up the Schatzberg Mountain. As everyone, apart from myself and one child, was unable to see clearly or not at all, the group moved slowly, with back-up and care being given without anyone being patronising. The Dorton House children were able to lead their seniors, an exercise that helped boost their self-esteem.

Figure 45. A feeling of pride having reached the top of the mountain

In turn, the elderly blind couple continued to be amazed by the confidence of these four young people. Similarly, other walkers turned to admire the purposeful group, many asking questions about where we came from. When children with visual handicaps are taken out and about and included in activities that might be thought to be beyond them, the rewards are innumerable. Sighted people walk in the rain on a mountain when the clouds are down. A blind boy who only felt the rain on his face was convinced he was walking 'through' a cloud. He will never forget his first experience of hard, cold conditions in the mountains. It might have put him off for life; but on the contrary, he wanted to return the next day for more, urging the rest of the group to go to bed early in preparation for an even longer walk.

When travelling out in the country and over hills or mountains, it is always useful to carry a small tape recorder. The children who are totally blind can then recall their day by listening again to the sounds of the grasshoppers, wind, water, birds, trees and machinery. As photographs jog the memories of the sighted, so sounds create just as much for the blind.

Above all, it is the joy of achieving something physical in such different surroundings from their normal lives that will stay with these children forever, this is clearly visible in photograph 45. If anyone feels that visually handicapped children are unable to cope with adverse conditions and hardships, I strongly disagree. I hope this description will help to prove how easy it is to achieve a great deal in a short time.

Similar expeditions to Austria took place in 1990 and 1991. On these trips the children who had been to Austria before matured and gave confidence to new members of the group. As soon as they reach the age of 14 these visually handicapped children will be able to complete the Bronze Expedition section of the Duke of Edinburgh Award Scheme with ease.

Further reading

Percy, M (1989) 'Journey Without An End' <u>Geographical Magazine</u>, April, 1989, 40-44

6

Two case studies that illustrate how visually impaired children can gain self-esteem through physical education and outdoor activities

This chapter aims to illustrate how physical and outdoor education can help to alleviate emotional and behavourial difficulties in two children who both attend a special school for the visually impaired.

Tim

Case study A is about Tim, an 11 year old boy who lost his sight when he was six months of age. He was diagnosed as having optic atrophy, which left him with a minimal amount of light perception in both eyes. Tim has always attended special schools for the visually handicapped.

Tim has a twin sister. He was born prematurely at 34 weeks, weighing 6.67 lbs. He and his twin sister remained in intensive care for two weeks after their birth and both babies were fully sighted. Between 0-6 months, Tim displayed slight developmental delay, which was attributed to his premature birth.

At six months Tim was blinded by an injury that caused bleeding behind both his eyes. As a result of this incident, both he and his sister were taken into care with different families. Tim is fostered and has remained with the same family all his life although they have not adopted him.

Tim first attended a special school for the visually handicapped when he was five years old and problems with his behaviour were first noticed by the staff at the school in year four. At his annual review in this year he was described as 'getting on well with adults.' His work was reasonable, especially his creative writing and use of vocabulary. He had begun to verbalise although his motor and self-help skills were considered to be poor. He took little interest in taking care of his own possessions and his mobility was hesitant and of a low standard. He rarely showed interest in moving on his own and frequently lapsed into the blind mannerisms of rocking and nodding his head. Although he was thought to have a good relationship with the other children, there were occasions when he lapsed into bad behaviour with them.

The following year he was thought generally to be happy by the staff, but lacking in motivation and maturity. His dressing and self-help skills were still poor and his motor skills were below average for a child of his age and visual disability. His foster parents and the school were unsure of the reason for his loss of ability in physical skills. The staff emphasised their concerns over his emotional behaviour. He used his creative writing to describe murders and killings and, on occasions, he was described as being domineering over other children by persuading them to misbehave and carry out rule-breaking and underhand activities. His behaviour was monitored and he was referred to an educational psychologist. He seemed to talk his way out of anything he found difficult in class. He was hesitant to move on his own in physical education lessons, as well as around the school and its grounds, except when he was given individual help.

When he was 11 years old, Tim joined a party of four junior children from his school who travelled to Austria. The party were accompanied by one member of staff, and stayed as guests of a family who run a hotel in the Tyrol. From the moment Tim knew he was being included in the party he began to channel his creative imagination into the adventure. His knowledge and interest in nature sparked off questions and projects about what he might feel, hear and meet whilst in Austria. The change in him was noticeable and his behaviour improved. He tried harder in physical education lessons in order to become fitter and he worked diligently at his swimming. Whilst in Austria he filled every moment of his time with intelligent questions and helpful comments. He was a popular member of the group. The outcome of this trip on his emotional problems is summed up in a report written by the member of staff who was in charge of him. The report was used by his educational psychologist and the school as proof that he was beginning to mature. His foster parents were delighted to know how well he had behaved whilst he was away.

Report

This report was made by the author following Tim's visit to Austria

TIM, aged 11 years

Tim had never flown before, but at Gatwick Airport and on the flight he took the procedure in his stride. He was one of three totally blind children in the group, and because of his poor mobility I kept him with me all the time around the airport on the outward journey. On coming home he did not need this support, and was accepted by the partially sighted child in the group as an easy friend to help.

From the moment we were picked up by our Austrian hosts at Munich, Tim was a sociable and lively member of the group. He settled in well to hotel life, and soon learnt to find his way around his large bedroom which he shared with another boy who has a minimal amount of sight. During the week he improved his dressing skills and, apart from the first two days, was up and dressed every morning before I went into the boys' room.

I noticed that over the week his rocking mannerisms became almost non-existent. I saw no evidence of violent talk, lying or gestures. He occasionally had to be told to stop and listen, instead of talking continuously.

During the week I was able to take the children into the mountains for over 30 hours walking. This, coupled with swimming, horse-riding and travelling about, made Tim physically tired. I noticed that his body became more relaxed, he walked without jerking and his arms dropped naturally to his sides. This is rarely apparent at school.

Tim is a bright child and he was able to find out a great deal about his surroundings by asking questions and listening. He has a good knowledge of bird calls and recognised many different species. He was eager to find out what slugs were and spent several afternoons collecting them from around the edges of the swimming pool surrounds for the hotel owners, as he knew they ate the lettuces in the garden. He gathered wild flowers with the others and helped to arrange them in a flower press.

Over the week Tim coped well at meal times. He knew what he wanted and did not over-eat. He handled his cutlery carefully, eating rather too close to the plate at times, but the chairs were on the low side for him.

I am certain that whilst he was with me in Austria he felt very happy. There was little or no evidence of any dissension between him and the group. On the walks, he was ready for more when the others had had enough. He insisted on swimming, whatever the weather. The weather is another of his obsessions, as is cricket. Knowing him as I do, I see these as genuine interests. The noise of a thunderstorm in the mountains is exciting for any child or adult for that matter.

I hope that on his return, Tim will be able to maintain the great improvement in his behaviour that he showed whilst away. He is a child who needs plenty of exercise, otherwise he will lapse back into unnecessary verbal descriptions of events instead of getting them out of his system by playing games, running, swimming or any other activity. These are always more difficult for the totally blind, but perfectly possible provided the activities are made exciting and enjoyable and there is a guaranteed level of success.

81

The benefit of Tim's greater confidence in himself stayed with him on his return to school. During the following school year, his swimming and physical education improved. He had greater powers of concentration in all his school work, although his natural exuberance at times got the better of him.

Twelve months later Tim was able to repeat his week in Austria. From the moment he left school until he returned a week later, the predictions proved to be correct. He continued where he had left off the previous year. He was very proud of the fact that he no longer need physiotherapy for his weak side. His right arm and leg had strengthened so much over the previous 12 months that he could now walk normally instead of dragging his right foot. He was the best motivated pupil on the mountain walks and this year collected sounds on his own portable dictaphone.

On his return he immediately settled down to writing a ten-page braille report on his travels which is given in precis below:

'Austrian Holiday'

This is my account of our trip to Austria. We woke up at 4 am the morning of departure, and we were taken in the school minibus to Gatwick airport. On arrival we checked in our luggage but a statue, a present for the Keller family (our hosts) made the x-ray machine bleep. We went to the departure lounge and waited for the plane. We boarded the plane on time and taxied along the runway. The air hostess went through the safety procedure in both German and English. I felt the strange sensations of take-off. We were on the plane for two hours before landing at Munich airport. Hans surprised us at passport control by creeping up behind us. By mistake Hans loaded me with the luggage on to the trolley. On loading the luggage into the bus Kerry's case burst open.

No more mishaps on the way. We hurtled round bends and down the hills. When we lurched to the right onto Kim and Sally and when we lurched again to the left, Sally and Kim fell on me.

When we arrived at the Kellerwirt everybody was overjoyed to see us and we unpacked and gave the Kellers their presents.

After lunch we walked up the Reidle Mountain. We stopped off at Mrs Walker's favourite red bench, and discussed what we were going to see when we went to the music school. On our return to the hotel, we had a shower, then we had our choice of supper, Weinersnitzel or fish. We then had a short constitutional walk before bed.

Day 2

Down to breakfast at half past eight then walking boots on, and on our way to the Kundle Klamm Gorge to listen to the secrets of the roaring torrent. On the way we saw the farmers busy at work. They were stacking up the hay. It was put onto great poles stretched across like a web from one pole to another. We saw the great wooden barn where the hay bales are stacked from floor to ceiling. It is a spectacular sight.

As we walked we heard the roaring wall of water getting closer and we saw how, as the gorge narrowed, water dropped away over the steep sides of the mountain. We saw some prehistoric leaves that the dinosaurs would have eaten a million years ago. They were all different shapes and sizes some in the shape of bowls, some in the shape of kites and so on. We also saw our first May Bug which is a type of beetle. There are 200 different varieties of beetles. May Bugs have claws which hook themselves to you. During the morning we drank out of a mountain stream. It was cold and refreshing.

In the evening we played with Rolf in Hans' garden. Rolf is the family Alsatian but in Austria they are known as German Shepherds. He is a big dog and very playful, and when I threw him the balls that I had brought for him he would run for them.

Towards the end of our evening with Rolf the heavens opened. We ran inside and sat in our beds listening to an exciting storm.

Day 3

We played near a stream, paddling and recording sounds.

Day 4

The Schatzberg Mountain. At 11.30 we went up in the gondola with Mr and Mrs Robinson. It was raining and I had to wear a tracksuit because it was cold. We felt the dizzy sensations on the gondola. It stopped off with a jerk. We could feel our tummies being pushed inwards and then it became smooth. We could hear the rain pounding on the metal roof and also a bit of hail. We got to the middle station and the door was burst open. We were going past the slopes where the people who are learning to ski, ski.

When we got to the top of the Schatzberg we stopped off at a mountain hotel and left the Robinsons in the sun (they have heart problems) whilst we climbed up to the top. On the way up we found pockets of snow. When we got to the cross at the top we stamped the walker's pass in our books. On the way down the Schatzberg the clouds started to close in. The atmosphere began to change to rain and we could not see anything. We were actually inside the clouds. There was a massive storm and we were hurt by huge hailstones. This was a new experience. Luckily for us we met two nice Germans who helped us down. We were taken to the hotel where the Robinsons were waiting and we had some hot chocolate.

When the weather had cleared up we went on another walk. We saw two shrines where people had died. Mrs Robinson liked the beautiful smell of the flowers.

We caught the bus home to Oberau and we were kindly presented with some Post Bus badges. However, when we got off the bus, the driver played a tune on his horn and an unsuspecting lady was so shocked that she dropped her shopping.

Day 5

Set off up rocky mountain path through the woods with the help of some friends. We heard many interesting sounds. First of all I heard a tree frog, it has a deep, whirring voice. We then, to our joy, heard a cuckoo which changes its tune in June to a little sad song. We then walked on a little further and sat down for a banana and a drink. We saw a farmer with his goats. We heard the tinkling of the bells.

The sound of bells was always with us through that exciting holiday particularly on that fifth day out in the wild mountains of Austria. All the time there was the comforting sound of birds wheeling and shrieking overhead. It was a nice atmosphere to have around us.

Day 6

Wednesday dawned bright and hot. This was the morning where we would have to prepare ourselves for when we went to the music School in Oberau.

We walked through the village to the school. The school is quite a big school. In Austria they start at 8 am and finish at 2 pm. Every week 7 hours of music get consumed. Their instruments are not the same because most instruments in Austria are Tyrolean. We felt and saw many different instruments.

When we got back to the Kellerwirt Hotel we made spaghetti and put on big chefs' hats and stirred the pot.

After lunch we set up an MBPS ('The May Bug Protection Service'). The aim of this was to fish out insects that had fallen into the swimming pool. In the evening we went to a Tyrolean Evening. The bit of the evening I liked best was when in the 'Miners Dance' the phosphorus was lit which went off with a bang!

Day 7

My 11th birthday. The day started well. I came down for breakfast. The table had been laid with sugar almonds, smarties, a happy birthday hat, a box of sweet cigarettes and chocolate, not counting my present from home.

After breakfast the MBPS was in full swing. We found one May Bug with an injured leg and 3-4 with wings missing. We had a jar with leaves and put the insects in. They depend on the wind to glide and fly up. When ours were dry we put them to our lips, blew and 'whoosh' they were away.

During the evening we played mini golf. It was an honourable draw. A perfect end to my birthday.

Day 8

The next day we said goodbye to our friends at the Kellerwirt and Hans drove us up to Munich airport. The flight home was a bumpy one which was delayed for a bit. But we have to agree we have had a thrilling holiday.

I gained much from this holiday. I learnt to be quicker over rocks and mountains and I feel more healthy, and I feel I have made a lot of people happy.

The End'

'I feel I have made a lot of people happy.' This is a statement from a well-adjusted, confident child. Physical activity can alleviate emotional difficulties in totally blind children. It provides a positive channel for their creative imaginations that might otherwise, through inactivty, be misused and so they are able to overcome difficulties that would otherwise require formal behaviour modification programmes.

It appears that physical exercise and positive motivation in the subjects that interest Tim eradicate his emotional problem. There are also direct suggestions that his academic work improved as a result. During his week in Austria he completed more mathematics, and English spelling and comprehension than he would have done in two weeks at school. In addition, he took an active part in all group activities, including the general diary that was written up by the only sighted child in the group. At the end of the summer term he was given two merit marks for his work, one for maths and the other for English.

Tim's foster parents noticed the change in him after his trip to Austria. Their feelings are illustrated in the letter his foster mother wrote the Principal of the school.

> 'I am writing to thank you for the superb trip to Austria. All the children enjoyed themselves I am sure, but more importantly Tim has gained an enormous amount of knowledge and experience as you will see from his written and taped report which he composed by himself'.

This increased confidence remained with him until the end of the school year. At the concert performed in front of Her Majesty the Queen, Tim sang and played the drums. Afterwards, the Queen personally congratulated him on his drumming.

Laura

Case study B is about Laura, a 15 year old, partially sighted girl. Laura attended mainstream sighted schools until she was 13.

Laura comes from a normal home background, the eldest of three girls. Her twin sister died in infancy. She is registered as partially sighted, suffering from nystagmus (rapid involuntary eye movements) and tunnel vision. She also has poor gross motor coordination resulting in clumsiness and poor mobility.

She attended sighted schools until she was 13 years old. It was felt at this time that her educational progress in a mainstream secondary school was very limited. She had become frustrated and lacked self-confidence. Her work was falling behind the standard of her year, so much so that special schooling was recommended. Despite being physically fit, she had difficulty with mobility and performing fine motor skills. She enjoyed disco dancing, ballet and tap. She also attended judo classes but quickly became frustrated if her progress was slow.

It was recommended by her mainstream school and the educational psychologist for the visually handicapped that she be transferred to a residential school for the visually handicapped. Her need for smaller classes and greater understanding of her visual disability would, it was felt, be catered for more easily amongst other visually handicapped children.

It took some time for her father to agree to Laura attending a residential special school; but her mother, who realised Laura's difficulties with self-help skills was in favour of the change from the start.

Laura's emotional difficulties did not disappear immediately she started as a weekly boarder at a residential school for the visually impaired. She continued to be selfish and demanding. She was found to be of below average academic ability.

Laura's frustration, and concern over her work resulted in emotional outbursts of prolonged crying, nervous anxiety and nightmares. Her constant night-time whimpering caused friction in her dormitory. She insisted on sleeping with a light on and this disturbed other partially sighted members of her boarding house group.

The standard of physical education at the school is high. Laura was able to take a full part in all school-based physical activities. Her expertise in dance and judo made her the best in her peer group, despite her shortened leg and pigeon toes (problems she has had since birth).

Her low academic achievement continued to cause worry. It was felt that she had little chance of taking external examinations except in music. This continued to depress her. The school kept in close contact with her parents throughout the school year.

In October 1987 Laura joined a school party taking part in mountain activities in the Brecon Beacons in Wales. Over the four days of the camp, Laura took a full part in every activity - hill walking, caving and campcraft. At night she slept on the floor of a barn, in total darkness, surrounded by the noise of mice and a few rats, with only another girl in her immediate vicinity. Whilst she was in Wales there was no sign of Laura's emotional difficulties, nightmares or phobias over light. She coped successfully with the physical side of the time away, finding sufficient energy and resources to help in the kitchen and to guide others who were totally blind.

A report written by the member of staff who accompanied the group sums up the success of introducing Laura to mountain activities.

Report

Laura, year 10

As Laura's form teacher this academic year, I have often noticed that she arrives at school in the morning in a state of emotional distress. This can take the form of hysterical crying or temper. Generally, she remains disturbed until lunchtime, meanwhile approaching individual members of staff in turn and seeking from them consolation and sympathy. She is not an academic pupil and has difficulty in keeping up with her peers in most subjects. This, in turn, causes great anxiety and frustration, as her marks are low.

In physical education she manages exceptionally well considering her slight physical disability. She enjoys working in the gym and outside. She perseveres with her swimming, which she does not find easy. She takes an active part in outdoor pursuits and copes with hill walking, caving and camping. This October, she came on a trip to Brecon for four days. During this time there was no sign of any distress and, above all, her obsession with light when sleeping, was not even mentioned. She slept for three nights on the floor of a barn, in total darkness, surrounded by the noises of mice and insects, with only one other girl for company, and made no request for even a torch.

On her return to school after this trip, Laura gradually managed to sleep without a light at night, much to the relief of her peers. The staff and her parents noticed during the rest of the 1987-1988 school year that her emotional outbursts were more spaced out. She became happier in herself and took a greater interest in organising her own belongings. She started, and completed, the bronze level of The Duke of Edinburgh's Award Scheme, having finished the expedition section in Wales earlier in the year.

In June 1989 her boarding house key worker (the boarding system had changed to family groups) reported that Laura seemed to have forgotten all about her night-time phobias. She had returned to Wales twice during the year, started sailing and continued with her dance and judo lessons. She was working hard for the Silver Standard Duke of Edinburgh's Award, selecting for her community service section, helping less able pupils at the school with their mobility, and a St John's Ambulance course. She was selected from 500 applicants to attend a cadet camp in Switzerland. She won her place from others owing to her experience in outdoor pursuits.

All children need to believe in themselves. Through physical and outdoor activities, Laura had proved to herself that, despite having a visual problem and a slight physical disability, she could achieve as much, if not more, than anyone else. She will never be an academic or find school work easy, but it is to be hoped that her interest in physical activities continues and gives her pleasure for the rest of her life.

The latest reports from her teachers and her key worker indicate that this improvement has been sustained. At the royal opening of the Further Education College at her school, she walked without fear, to her allotted place in the centre of the school assembly hall and note perfect, played Gershwin's 'Embraceable You' on her saxophone.

Although thought by many since the 1981 Education Act not to be the best for children with special needs (Hegarty et al (1987) and Dessent (1987)), special educational provision has its advantages. In an ordinary school, Tim's constant questions about the world around him would become trying for a mainstream teacher in charge of some 30 pupils. His physical difficulties, coupled with total blindness, might well exclude him from expeditions if he attended a mainstream school. Laura had tried to succeed in an ordinary school. Without extra assistance in the classroom, children with Laura's physical, educational and emotional handicaps are difficult to teach successfully.

Both these children have found positive parts of themselves through physical activities. Their levels of self-esteem have risen whilst in, or under mountains and they have carried the increased belief in themselves back to their everyday existence. It is to be hoped that all children with special needs will be included in the full range of physical education and outdoor activities. Apart from this being a compulsory part of the national curriculum, the rewards gained from worthwhile and exciting physical exercise are immeasurable.

Further reading

Hegarty, S. (1987) Meeting Special Needs in Ordinary Schools. London : Cassell

Dessent, T (1987) Making Ordinary Schools Special : Falmer Press

7

The End or the Beginning?

It is hoped that this book will dispel some of the doubts and concerns that physical educationists, especially those in mainstream schools, might have about including visually handicapped children in a variety of sports and physical activities. The aim of physical education today is to develop in all children a desire to continue to be active throughout their lives. Children who leave school without positive attitudes towards movement and physical exercise are unlikely to acquire active lifestyles as adults. Visually handicapped children face a greater risk of becoming sedentary than do their sighted peers. Pangrazi (1988) is worried that the present generation of obese children in America will grow into inactive, poorly-motivated adults, far more prone to heart disease and back problems than those who are taught to enjoy being healthy and fit when they are young. The dangers of visually handicapped children falling into this trap are far greater, especially if they are not exposed to a wide range of physical activities whilst at school.

The photographs in this book provide evidence that visually handicapped children can, and do, take part in and enjoy a wide range of physical education activities and outdoor pursuits. Most of the visually handicapped children in the photographs are past or present pupils at Dorton House School in Kent. At the time of writing the majority in the senior school are partially sighted and able to read print with the help of special equipment; relatively few are totally blind. In contrast, the junior school has more blind than partially sighted pupils. Having some sight makes mobility easier and should also make the inclusion of these children in mainstream physical activities easier.

It is not only the most able visually handicapped children who benefit from these activities. There are children at Dorton House School who have tumours, mild cerebral palsy, severe emotional and learning difficulties in additional to their visual impairment, who have all followed a full physical education programme and taken in part in outdoor pursuits.

Visually handicapped pupils attending mainstream schools who miss out on the physical education options offered in their schools, from a physical viewpoint would be better off receiving their movement education in a special school. This book has indicated ways and means to overcome the problems which mainstream physical educationists are likely to encounter if they include visually handicapped pupils in sighted PE classes. There will be times when further help is required. It is on these occasions that mainstream teachers should feel able to turn to special schools for assistance.

Bridging the gap between special and mainstream schools through physical education

The Warnock Report (1978) called for a much closer cooperation between special and ordinary schools including

> 'wherever possible the sharing of resources by pupils in both types of schools, and recommend that firm links should be established between special and ordinary schools in the same vicinity'.   DES, 1978, 8, 10

In physical education shared resources can be in the form of facilities such as gymnasia, sports halls, swimming pools and athletic tracks. Many special schools for visually handicapped pupils are well equipped and possess sports facilities that are superior to those in mainstream schools in their vicinity. It is possible to invite local schools to use the facilities at the special schools or to arrange joint activities. Special schools can use the facilities at local mainstream schools which may have larger swimming pools or be able to provide more opportunities for activities such as trampolining or weight training. As more schools opt for local management (LMS) it will be even more important for expensive sporting facilities to be shared if the National Curriculum requirements for physical education are to be achieved.

In Tunbridge Wells, pupils in a special school for children with learning difficulties, some of whom also have visual problems, use the next door comprehensive school's swimming pool. Dorton House's pool is used by local primary schools and several mainstream secondary schools. Younger children from local primary schools join in gymnastics and athletics in integrated clubs. With the introduction of the National Curriculum, it is important that links between special and ordinary schools become closer, to help ensure that all children with special educational needs have access to the full curriculum and opportunities to achieve their full potential.

Physical education teachers in mainstream schools must be made to feel welcome by staff in special schools. Information and advice can be given to mainstream schools through special schools' outreach services. 'Outreach' offered by special schools could, according to Galloway and Goodwin (1987), be regarded by some mainstream schools with sceptical mistrust. But special schools must not be seen as keeping their expertise closely guarded. It is not in their own interests to shut themselves away, with the misconceived idea that this will help them survive in the post-1981 integrationist educational climate. By sharing facilities and expertise, physical education departments in special schools could go a long way to dispel misconceived views, and most mainstream teachers who have to cope with children with special needs should welcome the chance to obtain practical advice.

The requirements for outreach services have arisen as a result of ordinary schools' obligations, since 1981, to make appropriate provision for pupils with special educational needs. Further, as a result of the 1980 Education Act and the 1988 Education Reform Act (ERA), all parents have the right to place their children in a school of their choice. This has given a greater incentive to parents with visually handicapped children to opt for an integrated setting. It is important for all physical education teachers in special schools for visually handicapped children to back mainstream teachers and to look on them as partners.

Links can be increased by making pupils in mainstream schools welcome to come into special schools as voluntary helpers. Mainstream children, especially those in the 4th, 5th and 6th years (years 10, 11 and 12), gain a great deal of pleasure and satisfaction from coming to help in special schools and units. Opportunities to work with children who have special needs benefit the helpers both socially and emotionally because, perhaps for the first time in their lives, they find others are totally dependent on them. On frequent occasions it is the mainstream helpers who come to Dorton House who benefit as much if not more, from the experience than the visually handicapped children. The care and thought that they put into their work is illustrated in the photographs. The extensive range of outdoor pursuits offered at Dorton House would not take place if local mainstream schools did not provide such help and assistance.

Special schools can also offer support services in physical education for visually handicapped children in mainstream schools. Camps similar to those arranged for visually handicapped children integrated into mainstream schools in America and Scandinavia, can be organised in this country. The aim of these would be to give the chance for visually handicapped pupils to meet others who understand and share their problems, and to receive extra help in subjects such as braille, typing, computer studies, physical activities and daily living skills.

Many visually handicapped people, both children and adults, welcome the chance to spend some time in their lives with other blind and partially sighted people. Living in the normal world with a visual handicap is a strain. A conversation with a 44 year old blind man who is a computer expert revealed that, despite continuing to live independently, travelling extensively in this country and abroad for his work, he welcomed the chance to talk to someone who understood some of his difficulties. Verbalising gestures comes naturally to those who work with visually handicapped people. This man said that time and again he had to ask others to say 'yes' or 'no' and not simply nod or shake their heads. Tobin and Hill (1988) reported in their study of 120 visually handicapped teenagers similar feelings and concerns about their visual problems.

Apart from offering visually handicapped pupils in mainstream schools a chance to catch up and 'socialise', a camp would give them the chance to experience living away from home, to have a holiday and perhaps find new interests.

A camp was organised at Dorton House School in August 1988. Ninety visually handicapped pupils between the ages of 13 - 18 from England, Denmark, Sweden and Holland lived and worked together for two weeks, experiencing physical education and outdoor pursuits.

The success of the camp was measured in the comments made by the students. On many occasions they said they were 'so excited to experience new activities.' They felt happy, they did not want to go home, and they 'could not wait for the next camp to be organised'. The Swedish group returned in 1990 to study languages. Biddle and Fox (1988) stressed the need to provide opportunities that

> 'lessen the impact of social comparison and provide skills focusing on personal improvement as achievement.'

Activity camps will achieve this aim.

Towards 2000: 'PE for All'

Physical education in schools today must be seen to cater for all children, especially those with special needs. Opportunities for out of school sport have declined. Fewer team games are being taught in schools and greater emphasis is being placed on individual fitness programmes. If this is true for children without disabilities, pupils with special needs must also be threatened. Brown (1987) is surely correct when he states that teachers of physical education must be prepared to 'individualise their teaching, evaluate their methods, and experiment with adaptive procedures'. Brown is referring to the teaching of games, but his message applies to the whole physical education programme for visually handicapped children.

Active life-styles increase the chance of visually handicapped pupils obtaining employment when they leave school. Industry requires school leavers to have developed 'body, mind and spirit' (Everard, 1988). Physical education can provide visually handicapped children with a sense of purpose, high self esteem and feelings of having positive identities, all necessary attributes for work.

Physical education programmes for visually handicapped children must include mobility skills and practice in orientation and spatial awareness. The ability to use the long cane, having the self-assurance to ask for help when it is needed and the confidence to travel independently, will increase the work prospects of all visually handicapped students. Physical education and

94

outdoor pursuits provide a means by which all children, especially those with a visual disability, can become fit, confident, self-assured adults.

With this sharing of problems between special and mainstream schools, it is to be hoped that by the year 2000 all visually handicapped children whether in special or mainstream schools, will be able to look back on their physical education at school and say

'THAT WAS FUN!'

Further Reading

Ainscow, M (1989) 'Developing the Special School Curriculum' In : Baker, D and Bovair, K (Eds) (1989) <u>Making the Special Schools Ordinary?</u> <u>Volume 1</u>. Lewis : Falmer Press

Biddle, S and Fox, K (1988) 'The Child's Perspective in Physical Education Part 4 : Achievement and Psychology' <u>British Journal of Physical Education</u>, 19, 4-5, 182-185

Brown, A (1987) 'The Integration of Children with Movement Problems Into the Mainstream Games Curriculum' <u>British Journal of Physical Education</u>, 18, 5, 230-232.

Department of Education and Science (DES) (1978) <u>The Education of the Visually Handicapped</u> (Vernon Report) London : HMSO

Department of Education and Science (DES) (1988) <u>Education Reform Act</u>
London : HMSO

Everard, B (1988) 'The Contribution of Physical Activities to the Education and Training of Young People : A view from outside the profession' <u>British Journal of Physical Education</u>, 19, 2, 64-65

Galloway, D and Goodwin, C (1987) <u>The Education of Disturbing Children</u>. London : Longman

Murdoch, H (1987) <u>Sport in Schools</u> London : Department of Education and Science (DES)

Pangrazi, R P (1988) 'Physical Education in the Primary Schools' <u>British Journal of Physical Education</u>, 19, 4-5, 149-151

Tobin, M J and Hill, E W (1989) 'The present and the future : concepts of visually impaired teenagers' <u>British Journal of Visual Impairment</u>, VIII, 2, 55-57

Appendix 1

Additional reading

Adkins, P G and Ainsa T D (1979) 'An Early Stimulation Programme for Visually Handicapped Infants and Toddlers' Education of the Visually Handicapped, X, 2, 75-79

Barraga, N C (1976) Visual Handicaps and Learning -A Developmental Approach. USA : Wadsworth Publishing Company

Barraga, N (1983) Visual Handicaps and Learning : Revised Edition. Houston : Exceptional Resources

Biddle, S J H (1984) 'Attribution Theory in Sport and Recreation : Origins, Developments and future directions' Physical Education Review, 7, 145-159

Care, C (1988)'The Changing Face of Outdoor Education' British Journal of Physical Education, 19,2, 52-54

Carriage, E (1986) 'Not a "Soft Option"' British Journal of Physical Education, 22, 1, 15-21

Chapman, E K, Tobin, M J, Tooze, F G H, Moss, S C (1987) Look and Think : A handbook on Visual Perception Training for Severely Visually Handicapped Children. London : Schools Council. (revised edition RNIB 1989)

Chin, D L (1988) 'Dance Movement Instruction : Effects on Spatial Awareness in Visually Impaired Elementary Students' Journal of Visual Impairment and Blindness, 82, 5, 188-192

Collins, M E Barraga, N C (1980) 'Development of efficiency in visual functioning : An evaluation process' Journal of Visual Impairment and Blindness, 74, 3-96

Cotton, M (1983) Outdoor Adventure for Handicapped People London : Souvenir Press

Conway, D Green, M and Zaluchi, M (1982) 'Physical Education, Recreation and Extra-Curricular Activities with Visually Impaired' In : Hanninen, K A (Ed) (1982) The Horizons of Blindness Michigan : Blindness Publications

Craft, D (1986) 'Curricular Adaptions, Physical Education' In : Scholl, G T (Ed) (1986) <u>Foundations of Education for the Blind and Visually Handicapped Youth.</u> New York : American Foundation for the Blind.

Crosbie, R J (1980) 'The Partially Sighted Child In the Secondary School' In : Harvey, D J (Ed) (1980) Children Who Are Partially Sighted. Birmingham : AEWVH

Day, A (1989) 'Reaching Out : The Background to Outreach' In : Baker, D and Bovair, K. (Eds) (1989) <u>Making the Special Schools Ordinary.</u> Volume 1. London : Falmer Press

Derrick, R (1988) 'Plucky Pupils' <u>Education</u> 22 April, 354-356

Dobree, J H and Boulter, E (1982) <u>Blindness and Visual Handicap</u> Oxford : Oxford University Press

Dryhurst, B, Spencer, C, and Baybutt, K (1987) 'The Evaluation of a training programme in orientation skills' <u>British Journal of Visual Impairment,</u> 111, 2, 41-43

Duggar, M (1968) 'What can dance be to someone who cannot see?' <u>Journal of Health, Physical Education and Recreation,</u> 39, 30-38

Edwards, A (1989) 'Identity construction and schooling' In : Reid, K. (Ed) (1989) <u>Helping Troubled Pupils in secondary Schools.</u> <u>Volume 1</u> Oxford : Blackwell Education

Evans, B and Simmons, K (1987) 'Exercises in Integration' <u>British Journal of Special Education,</u> 14, 3, 115-117

Frostig, M and Maslow, P (1970) <u>Movement Education : Theory and Practice</u> Chicago:Follett

Hatlen, P H and Curry, S A (1987) 'In Support of Specialized Programs for Blind and Visually Impaired Children : The Impact of Vision Loss On Learning' <u>Journal of Visual Impairment and Blindness,</u> 81, 1, 7-13

Hegarty, S (1987) <u>Meeting Special Needs in Ordinary Schools.</u> London : Cassell

Higgins, B (1987) 'Building Bridges Between Mainstream And Special Schools' <u>British Journal of Physical Education,</u> 18, 5, 221-222

Hill, E W (1986) 'Orientation and Mobility' In : School, G T (ED) (1986) <u>Foundations of Education for Blind and Visually Handicapped Children.</u> New York : American Foundation for the Blind.

Hill, E and Blach, B B (1980) 'Concept Development' In : Welsh, R L and Blach, B B (1980) <u>Foundations of Orientation and Mobility</u>. New York : American Foundation for the Blind.

Hodgson, A (1985) 'Meeting Special Needs in Mainstream Classrooms' <u>British Journal of Special Education</u>, 12, 3, 117-118

Jamieson, M Parlett, M, Pocklington, K (1977) <u>Towards Integration : A Study of Blind and Partially Sighted Children in Ordinary Schools.</u> Windsor: NFER-Nelson

Jan, J E, Freeman, R D and Scott, E P (1977) <u>Motor Development, Posture and Physiotherapy</u>. New York : Grune and Stratton

Joffee, E (1988) 'A Home-Based Orientation and Mobility Program for Infants and Toddlers' <u>Journal of Visual Impairment and Blindness</u>, 82, 7, 282-285

Jose, R T (Ed) (1983) <u>Understanding Low Vision</u>. New York : American Foundation for the Blind.

Meighan, R (1988) <u>Flexischooling: Education for Tomorrow, Starting Today</u>. Ticknall : Education Now Publishing Cooperative

Michalsen, P M and Sterm. R J (1982) 'Parent Attitude and Preschool Intervention with Blind Children' In : Hanninen, K A (Ed) (1982) <u>The Horizons of Blindness</u>. Michigan : Blindness Publications

McNeill, C Ramsden, J, Renfrew, T (1986) <u>Teaching Orienteering</u>. Doune : Harveys.

Parker, J (1988) 'Decision Making In Outdoor Education' <u>Adventure Education</u>, 5, 1, 13-15

Parker, T (Ed) (1970) <u>An Approach to Outdoor Activities</u>. London : Palham Books

Parker, T M and Meldrum, K I (1973) <u>Outdoor Education</u> London : J Dent.

Petrucci, D (1953) 'The Blind Child and His Adjustment' <u>New Outlook For the Blind</u>, 47, 8, 240-246

Pointer, B (1989) <u>Gym and Tonic - successful integration through PE'.</u> <u>Bulletin of Physical Education</u>, 25, 2, 13-15

Potter, L (1987) 'Letter To The Editor' <u>Journal of Visual Impairment and Blindness</u>, 81, 10, 459.

Price, R J (1980) Physical Education and the Physically Handicapped Child. London : Lepus Books.

Roberts, C (1988) Go For It. Melbourne : Oxford University Press.

Roberts, T (1970) 'Rock Climbing' In : Parker, T (Ed) (1970) An Approach to Outdoor Activities. London : Pelham

Russell, J P (1988) Graded Activities For Children With Motor Difficulties. Cambridge : Cambridge University Press

Shakespeare, R (1975) The Psychology of Handicap. London : Methuen

Silver, J Gould, E (1976) 'A Study of Some Factors Concerned in the Schooling of Visually Handicapped Children' Child : Care, Health and Development, 2, 145-153

Sonksen, P M Levitt, S and Kitzinger, M (1984) 'Identification of constraints acting on motor development in young visually disabled children and principles of remediation' Child : Care, Health and Development, 10, 273-286

Terzieff, I S (1988) 'Visual Impairments' In : Lynch, E W and Lewis, R B (Eds) (1988) Exceptional Children and Adults; Boston : Scott, Foresman and Company.

Tooze, D (1967) 'Mobility for the Junior Blind Child' Teacher of the Blind, V, 4 108-111.

Tuttle, D W (1987) 'The Role of the Special Education Teacher Counsellor in Meeting Students' Self-Esteem Needs' Journal of Visual Impairment and Blindness, 81, 4, 156-161.

Walker, J (1989) 'Helping pupils from unsupportive home backgrounds : divorce' In : Reid, K (Ed) (1989) Helping Troubled Pupils in Secondary Schools. Volume One. Oxford : Blackwell.

Ward, C (1980) 'The Partially Sighted Child In The Primary School' In : Harvey, D J (Ed) (1980) Children Who Are Partially-Sighted. Birmingham : Association for the Education and Welfare of the Visually Handicapped (AEWVH)

Warren, D H (1984) Blindness and Early Childhood Development, 2nd Edition, Revised. New York : American Foundation for the Blind

Wetton, P (1988) Physical Education in the Nursery and Infant School. London : Croom Helm

White, M (1980) 'Mobility And The Partially Sighted' In : Harvey, D J (Ed) (1980) <u>Children Who Are Partially Sighted</u>. Birmingham : AEWVH.

Whitehead, E (1988) 'Travelling Blind' <u>The Adventurers</u>, 1, 2, 18

Williams, D (1984) 'Children with Special Needs' <u>Bulletin of Physical Education,</u> 20, 2, 43-53

Wilson, J (1987) 'How can PE promote an active lifestyle?' <u>British Journal of Physical Education</u>, 18, 2, 53-54.

Wilson, M (1987) 'Schools : An Evolutionary View' <u>Special Education : Forward Trends</u>, 5, 3, 14-16.

Woodhouse, J (1988) 'Outdoor Activities - Establishing A life-Long Friendship' <u>Bulletin of Physical Education</u>, 23, 3, 9-13.

Appendix 2

Organisations and services

Activity Holidays
Details of group activity holiday courses are available from RNIB Leisure Service, 224 Great Portland Street, London W1N 6AA Tel 071 388 1266

Archery
Grand National Archery Society, Disabled Archery Coordinator, National Agricultural Centre, Stoneleigh, Kenilworth, Warwicks CV8 2LG
Tel 0203 696631

British Blind Sport (BBS), Administrative and Development Officer, 67 Albert Street, Rugby, Warwickshire Tel 0788 536142

British Sports Association for the Disabled, (BSAD)
34 Osnaburgh Street, London NW1 3ND Tel 071 383 7277

Canoeing
British Canoe Union, John Dudderidge House, Adbolton Lane, West Bridgford, Nottinghamshire NG2 5AS Tel 0602 821100

Chess
Braille Chess Association, (BCS), Hon. Sec. Mr S. Lovell, 7 Coldwell Square, Cross Gates, Leeds LS15 7HB Tel 0532 600013

British Chess Federation, 9A Grand Parade, St Leonards-on-Sea, East Sussex TN38 ODD Tel 0424 442500

Churchtown Farm Field Studies Centre
Lanlivery, Bodmin, Cornwall PL30 5BT Tel 0208 872148

Duke of Edinburgh's Award Scheme, Gulliver House, Madeira Walk, Windsor, Berkshire Tel 0753 810753

Football
British Football Association for the Visually Handicapped, (BFAVH), Chairman, 1 Malvern Close, Prestwick, Manchester M25 5PH

Girl Guides Association, 17-19 Buckingham Palace Road, London SW1W OPT Tel 071 834 6242

Goalball Association, 51 Sarnway, Darley Abbey, Derbyshire DE3 2BQ
Tel 0332 559172

Golf
English Blind Golf,, 93 St Barnabas Road, Woodford Green, Essex IG8 7BT
Tel 081 505 2085

The Golf Foundation, 57 London Road, Enfield EN2 6DU Tel 081 367 4404

Guide Dog Adventure Group (GDBA), Hillfields, Burghfield Common,
Reading, Berkshire RG7 3YG Tel 0734 835555

Gymnastics
British Amateur Gymnastics Association, Thames Valley College,
Wellington Street, Slough, Berkshire SL1 1XT Tel 0753 534171

Holidays for the Disabled, (Young Disabled on Holiday), 12 Ryle Road,
Farnham GU99 8RW Tel 0252 721390

Holiday Care Service, 2 Old Bank Chambers, Station Road, Horley, Surrey
RH6 9HW Tel 0293 774535

Horse-riding/pony-trekking
Riding for the Disabled Association (RDA), Secretary, Avenue 'R', National
Agricultural Centre, Kenilworth, Warwicks CV8 2LY Tel 0203 696510

Island Cruising Club, Dinghy Master, The Island, Salcombe, South Devon
TQ8 8DR Tel 0548 843481

Outward Bound Trust, (HQ Office), Chestnut Field, Regent Place, Rugby
CV21 2PJ Tel 0788 60423

Rowing
Amateur Rowing Association, (Rowing for the Disabled), 6 Lower Mall,
Hammersmith, London W6 9DJ   Tel 071 748 3632

Sailing
Jubilee Sailing Trust, Test Road, Eastern Docks, Southampton SO1 1GG
Tel 0703 631388

Scout Association, Gilwell Park, Chingford, London E4 7QW
Tel 071 524 5246

Rambling
The Ramblers Association, Secretary, 1-5 Wandsworth Road, London SW8
2XX Tel 071 582 6878

Royal Yachting Association (RYA) Seamanship Foundation, Director,
22/24 Romsey Road, Eastleigh, Hampshire SO5 4AL Tel 0703 629962

Ski-ing
British Ski Club for the Disabled (BSCD), 'Springmount', Berwick St John, Shaftesbury, Dorset SP7 OHQ

Swimming
Amateur Swimming Association, Secretary, Harold Fern House, Derby Square, Loughborough, Leics. LE11 OAL   Tel 0509 230431

Tandem Cycling
The Tandem Club, Liaison Officer for the Visually Handicapped, Worlds End House, 56 High Street, Green Street Green, Kent BR6 6BJ

Trampolining
British Trampoline Federation Ltd, Secretary, 146 College Road, Harrow, Middlesex HA1 1VH   Tel 081 863 7278

Water ski-ing
British Disabled Water-ski Association (BDWSA), The Tony Edge Centre, Heron Lake, Hythe End, Wraysbury TW9 6HW 0784 483664

Youth Hostels Association, (England and Wales), Trevelyan House, 8 St Stephen's Hill, St Albans, Herts AL1 2DY   Tel 0727 55215

Appendix 3

Publications

Directory of Scented Gardens and Gardens for Blind/Disabled People
(23 pp), Royal National Institute for the Blind (1984), from: RNIB Leisure
Service, 224 Gt Portland Street, London W1N 6AA Tel 071 388 1266 (£1.25).

Directory of Nature Trails for Visually Handicapped People (31 pp), RNIB
(1984), from: RNIB Leisure Service (£1.25)

Games for Deaf-Blind Children Joan Shields (2 pp), RNIB (1983), from
RNIB Leisure Service (free)

Leisure for all - Opportunities for visually handicapped people, RNIB
(1990), from RNIB Production and Distribution Centre, PO Box 173,
Peterborough PE2 6WS Tel 0733 370777 (£3.50)

Participation membership magazine available in print and tape from British
Blind Sport, annual subscription £5.00

RNIB Games & Puzzles Product Guide (+price list), RNIB (1991), from
RNIB Production and Distribution Centre, PO Box 173, Peterborough
PE2 6WS (free)

Sport for Visually Handicapped People: Two Perspectives, C Attrill and
J Deaper, (Supplement - two lists of activities) (6 pp), RNIB (1981) and
British Sports Association for the Disabled, Southern Region (1983), from
RNIB Leisure Service (free)

Sport, **Recreation**, (for the blind) and **Sport and PE for blind children**,
from: RNIB Reference Library

Some Considerations for teaching PE to Children with Impaired Sight,
D Wood (1987), (7 pp) from RNIB Leisure Service (free)

Swimming for the Disabled, Association of Swim Therapy (146 pp), (1981),
from: A & C Black Ltd, (Publishers), 35 Bedford Row, London WC1R 4JH
(£4.95)

They said we couldn't do it (51 pp) (Sailing), RYA Seamanship Foundation
(1981), from: Royal Yachting Association (£1.00)

The Enjoyment of Gardens by Blind and Partially Sighted People (8 pp),
South Regional Association for the Blind (1979), from: SRAB, 55 Eton
Avenue, Swiss Cottage, London NW1 3ET and RNIB Leisure Service (free)

Textbook of Sport for the Disabled, Sir L Guttmann (184 pp), (1976), from: H M & M Publishers Ltd, Milton Road, Aylesbury, Bucks. (£14.95)

Toys

Toys with a Purpose, (July 1980) : 7 page leaflet, available from RNIB Education & Leisure Division, 224 Great Portland Street, London W1N 6AA Tel 071 388 1266

What Toy, published by CT Publications, (£2.45), available from Play Matters, National Toy Libraries Association, 68 Churchway, London NW1 1LT Tel 071 387 9592

Schools and colleges for blind and partially sighted pupils in the UK

Clapham Park School, 127 Park Hill, Clapham, London, SW4 9PA, Tel: 081 674 5639, Lambeth LEA; some pupils with additional learning difficulties; ages 3-16 years

Dorton House School, Seal, Sevenoaks, Kent TN15 OED, Tel: 0732 61477, Royal London Society for the Blind; boarding/day; some pupils with additional learning difficulties; ages 4-16 years

Exhall Grange School, Wheelwright Lane, Exhall, Coventry CV7 9HP, Tel: 0203 364200, Warwickshire LEA; boarding/day; some pupils with additional learning difficulties; ages 3-19 years

George Auden School, Bell Hill, Northfield, Birmingham B31 1LD, Tel: 021 475 3826, City of Birmingham LEA; day; some pupils with additional learning difficluties; ages 2-12 years

Henshaw's College, Bogs Lane, Starbeck, Harrogate, North Yorkshire HG1 4ED, Tel: 0423 886451, independent/non-maintained; boarding/day; some pupils with additional learning difficulties; ages 11-19 years

Jordanstown Schools, 85 Jordanstown Road, Newtownabbey Co Antrim BT37 0QE, Tel: 0232 863541, voluntary maintained; boarding/day; some pupils with hearing impairment; ages 3-17+ years

Joseph Clarke School, Vincent Road, Highams Park, Chingford E4 9PP Tel: 081 527 8818, Waltham Forest LEA; some pupils with additional learning difficulties; ages 2-19 years

Kaimes School, 140 Lasswade Road, Edinburgh, EH16 6RT Tel: 031 664 8241, Lothian LEA; day; partially sighted; some pupils with additional learning difficulties; ages 5-17 years

Kelvin School, 69 Nairn Street, Glasgow G3 8SE, Tel: 031 339 5839 Strathclyde LEA; day; nursery unit for blind and partially sighted, also some pupils with additional learning difficulties; primarily partially sighted pupils; ages 5-16+ years

Linden Lodge School, 61 Princes Way, Wimbledon Park, London SW19 6JB, Tel: 081 788 0107, Wandsworth LEA; boarding/day; pupils with both vision and hearing loss; ages 5-16 years

Priestley Smith School, Perry Common Road, Birmingham B23 7AT
Tel: 021 373 5493, City of Birmingham LEA; day; some pupils with additional learning difficulties; ages 2-17 years

RNIB Condover Hall School, Condover, Shrewsbury, Shropshire SY5 7AH, Tel: 074 3722320, RNIB; day/boarding; school for pupils with additional learning difficulties; ages 5-19 years

RNIB Sunshine House School, Dunnings Road, East Grinstead, West Sussex RH19 4ND, Tel: 0342 323141, RNIB; boarding/day; some children with additional learning difficulties; ages 2-8 years

RNIB Sunshine House School, Dene Road, Northwood, Middlesex HA6 2DD Tel: 0923 822538, RNIB; day/boarding; some pupils with additional learning difficulties; ages 2-8 years

RNIB Sunshine House School, 2 Oxford Road, Birkdale, Southport, Merseyside PR8 2JT. Tel: 0704 67174, RNIB; day/boarding; some pupils with additional learning difficulties; ages 2-8+ years

RNIB New College Worcester, Whittington Road, Worcester WR5 2JU Tel: 0905 763933, RNIB; day/boarding; school for pupils following a broad academic curriculum leading to Higher and Further Education; ages 11-18 years

Royal School for the Blind, Church Road North, Wavertree, Liverpool L15 6TQ Tel: 051 733 1012, Registered charity administered by a committee of management; day/boarding; some pupils with additional learning difficulties; ages 5-19 years

Shawgrove School, Cavendish Road, West Didsbury, Manchester M20 8JR, Tel: 061 445 9435, City of Manchester LEA; day; some pupils with additional learning difficulties; ages 3-16 years

St Vincent's School for the Blind and Partially Sighted
Yew Tree Lane, West Derby, Liverpool L12 9HN, Tel 051 228 9968, Independent; day/boarding; some pupils with additional learning difficulties; ages 4-17 years

St Vincent's School for the Blind, Deaf and Partially Sighted 30 Fullarton Avenue, Tollcross, Glasgow G32 8NT Tel: 041 778 2254 Strathclyde LEA; boarding/day; ages 5-18 years

Tapton Mount School, 20 Manchester Road, Sheffield S10 5DG Tel: 0742 667151, Sheffield LEA; boarding/day; some pupils with additional learning difficulties; pupils of secondary age may be considered for an Open Education Integrated Scheme within Tapton Secondary School; ages 4-12 years

Temple Bank School for the Visually Impaired, Daisy Hill Lane, Bradford, West Yorkshire, BD9 6BN, Tel: 0274 541714, Bradford LEA; some pupils with additional learning difficulties; ages 2-19 years

The Royal Blind School, Craigmillar Park, Edinburgh EH16 5NA
Tel: 031 667 1100, Royal Blind Asylum; boarding' public examinations and professional training; ages 3-19 years and **Canaan Lodge**, Multi-handicapped Department, Canaan Lane, Edinburgh EH10 4SG

Whitefield School & Centre, MacDonald Road, Walthamstow, London E17 4AZ Tel: 081 531 3426, Waltham Forest LEA; boarding/day; pupils with both vision and hearing loss; ages 2-19 years

Ysgol Penybont for Visually Handicapped Children, Ewenny Road, Bridgend, Mid-Glamorgan, S. Wales, CF31 3HT, Tel: 0656 653974, Mid-Glamorgan LEA; boarding/day; some pupils with additional learning difficulties; ages 5-16 years

Colleges for Visually Impaired Students

Dorton College of Further Education, Seal Drive, Seal, Sevenoaks, Kent TN15 OAH Tel: 0732 61477, Royal London Society for the Blind; boarding/day; some pupils with additional learning difficulties; ages 16+

Queen Alexandra College, 49 Court Oak Road, Harborne, Birmingham B17 9TG Tel: 021 427 4577, BRIB; day/residential; some students with additional learning difficulties; vocational courses in engineering; cycle mechanics; telephone/reception; information processing; light assembly; links with other Further Education colleges for other courses; rehabilitation; counselling; national certification; ages 16-55 years

Royal National College and Academy of Music for the Blind, College Road, Hereford HR1 1EB Tel: 0432 265725; Independent; residential; foundation course; GCSE; A Levels; business studies; computer programming; piano tuning. The college also acts as an assessment centre for visually impaired students going into further education; ages 16+ years

RNIB Hethersett College, Philanthropic Road, Redhill, Surrey, RH1 4DZ, Tel: 0737 768935, RNIB; day/residential college offering pre-vocational and vocational education, and training in living skills; ages 16+ years

RNIB Vocational College, Radmoor Road, Loughborough, Leics. LE11 3BS; Tel: 0509 611077, RNIB; day/residential college in partnership with Loughborough College; offers shorthand; typing; audio-typing; telephony; information processing; computer programming; use of special aids to employment and access with support to courses at the mainstream Loughborough College; ages 16+ years